THE 7 NAVIGATORS

How to Pilot Your Life

Steve Hartfield

The 7 Navigators: How To Pilot Your Life

Copyright © 2019 Steve Hartfield

ISBN: 9781688651906

All rights reserved. No portion of this book may be reproduced mechanically, electronically, or by any other means, including photocopying, without permission of the publisher or author except in the case of brief quotations embodied in critical articles and reviews. It is illegal to copy this book, post it to a website, or distribute it by any other means without permission from the publisher or author.

Limits of Liability and Disclaimer of Warranty
The author and publisher shall not be liable for your misuse of the enclosed material. This book is strictly for informational and educational purposes only.

Warning – Disclaimer
The purpose of this book is to educate and entertain. The author and/or publisher do not guarantee that anyone following these techniques, suggestions, tips, ideas, or strategies will become successful. The author and/or publisher shall have neither liability nor responsibility to anyone with respect to any loss or damage caused, or alleged to be caused, directly or indirectly by the information contained in this book.

Publisher
10-10-10 Publishing
Markham, ON
Canada

Printed in Canada and the United States of America

Contents

Dedication — v
Foreword — vii
Acknowledgements — ix
Introduction: A Changing World — xiii

Chapter 1: Wisdom — 1
Chapter 2: Understanding — 13
Chapter 3: Counsel — 29
Chapter 4: Might — 43
Chapter 5: Knowledge — 59
Chapter 6: Fear of your Creator — 75
Chapter 7: The Spirit of Your Creator — 91
Chapter 8: Cruising Altitude — 107

Conclusion — 123

I dedicate this book to every youth, young adult, and veteran who is looking to find their place in this world. The greatest journey starts within, and it is my hope that you find clarity.
With God, all things are possible!

Foreword

Are you looking for answers for your purpose in life? Do you have trouble figuring out your natural strengths and talents? Do you love learning about yourself and the people around you?

No matter your current estimation of yourself, you are a wonderful and carefully made person, and you are here to create something that will astonish the world! Now is the time to discover who you truly are and take action to uncover your spiritual self.

As a veteran of the United States Air Force, author Steve Hartfield has committed his life to serving others and teaching the importance of spiritual enlightenment. He has taught hundreds of people within the Christian and Spiritual communities about finding their true purpose in life, encouraging them to seek their unique path to self-fulfillment. He can do the same for you.

The world can be a confusing place, and you may feel discouraged about expressing yourself in your own special way. Steve has written this book as a sign of hope, to show you what is available if you become aware of your role in the universe. It is my hope that you find this book as enjoyable as I have, and that it opens your mind to what is possible within your life.

Raymond Aaron
New York Times Bestselling Author

Acknowledgements

I would like to thank my mother, **Pamela J Hartfield**. She is the angel that has guided me and loved me unconditionally to enable me to become the man I am today. When I was at my lowest point in life, you saw history in the making, and willed me to keep working hard and stay strong in my battles.

Taylor R Wilson, for being a kind and loving sister who, from the day she was born, has supported our mother. We are tied together for a reason beyond our understanding, and the seeds of our love are growing each time I see you.

Ronald E Hartfield, for loving me in the best way that he saw possible. His journey in life has been my inspiration to see the world in a new way, with patience and a sense of reality.

Nathan Hartfield Sr. and Hattie Hartfield, for being the patriarchs of this family. I can't think of two other spirits that I have come across that have set so much in motion for the lives and legacy of so many other people.

Tim, Toni, Khari, Todd and **Kayla Woods,** for showing me the excellent example of how a faith-filled family is supposed to live life. From the time Tim helped raise me, to seeing the kids walk in the same anointing, it has been a blessing.

Nathan Hartfield Jr. and Karl Hartfield, for being the leaders of our family after Grandfather's passing. There is nothing we can do to pay you back for the responsibility on your shoulders to get our family where we are. And for that, I thank you.

Bernard Hartfield, Edward Thomas, and the brothers of **Omega Psi Phi, Fraternity Inc.**, for showing me the values of manhood, scholarship, perseverance, and uplift are embedded in our daily lives as we aspire for excellence. Friendship is truly essential to the soul.

Mae Ora Sommers, for being the beacon of life for my mother, showing her what hard work and perseverance meant in such a troubling time in our community.

Nathan III, Reginald, Tiffany, and Karen Hartfield, for showing me unending love from the time I was born. The support system you have provided is priceless, and the lives you live are special in their own way.

Acknowledgements

Patricia Bratcher, Claudette Lewis, Top Teens of America and the Cherice Cochrane Foundation, for empowering me with the core fundamentals of leadership and diplomacy at such a young age in my development as a leader. The lessons you have taught me still apply to my growth and development as a man today.

The members of **St. Luke Baptist Church** and **New Mount Pleasant MBC**, there is no way that I could possibly have received the word of God and teachings of my Lord and Savior without the love and support that both churches have shown me. For that, I am forever grateful.

Gloria and Rosie Dees, for providing my first home, and sense of family, in the newest chapter of my life. God connects spirits for a reason, and you have indeed saved my life and are keeping me on the right path to live the life I didn't see as possible.

Linda Hartfield, Stella Brown, and Ramona Wesley, for your guidance and love for me throughout my life. God bless you for everything you are and the love you share with the world.

Introduction: A Changing World

Each generation has battles they must fight that are relevant for their time and age. After the year 2003, when the first iPhone came, children were born every year where they did not know life outside smartphone technology. A lot of the biggest challenges comes with the flood of information that we face, which has created an artificial connection between us and the world, reducing our social interaction skills to a dangerously low level. But the idea is that as the world changes, we must evolve on how we process information, and embrace challenges in a new way. It will take a while for our generation to become educated on the simple lessons of discipline and hard work, since so much information gives us the ability to change course so frequently. But once we understand the lasting lessons of wisdom that have been given to us from previous generations and apply them in a new way in this new century, we will be able to progress from the 20th century, to make our own impact on the world.

We lose sensitivity when we are too engaged in the screens of the world, because we miss the true beauty in life, and each passing moment flies over our heads without any hesitation. Once we can gain awareness of the reasons why we must escape to our smartphones, then we can begin to enjoy the simple pleasures of the present. It is important to realize that the humanness of life will not give us an exciting moment that we visualize in our minds all the time, but understand that an endless fountain of knowledge lies in every person and every environment that we have the privilege of being placed in.

We always have faith in the pilot to get us to our destination, without even meeting the person, because we trust that the airline that we gave our money to provided the proper training and mentorship to the captain and crew. We must have the same applied faith when it comes to piloting our own lives, because every moment that you have been placed into, the Universe has given you the proper training to handle the moment, regardless of the joy or pain it possesses. Every person has a *"true-self"* within them, which is hidden until the time comes for them to have the choice of bringing it out or keeping it hidden from the world. This is your confirmation to let your true-self out, in order to be able to take control again and stop being a victim of the circumstances that come into your life.

One of the first lessons that we can learn from our teenage years is the fact that we don't know what we don't know, and everyone in this world is trying to figure things out just like we are, and we can be confident that the right choices come once we learn how to be still, and feel for the answer within our own minds. The idea of feeling for the right choices comes with having a calm mind. Before you can leave the runway, it will be important that you learn that all decisions don't have to be made in a hurry, and we all have an inner conscious that will lead us in the appropriate direction.

Introduction: A Changing World

The narrative is not over for generation Y and the hidden capabilities within people in the next few decades, but it is time that we use the skills and awareness of the world that we have, and seek new information to give us the tools to take off from the runway and guide our lives confidently into the unknown world.

Chapter 1

Wisdom

"Love and desire are the spirit's wings to great deeds."
– Johann Wolfgang von Goethe

What Are The 7 Navigators?

In short, it is a spiritual guide. When a pilot is preparing an airplane for flight, they must clear a pre-flight checklist—items that are necessary for the plane's internal controls, fuel, and flying conditions—in order to be cleared for flight. Within the context of this book, these are the things you must know about yourself before you embark on a journey, because in order to do something in life, you have to know who you are—your strengths, your talents, your support system—and know about your passion. And once you take off, you have to learn how to get to the top and reach *cruising altitude*—where you can go anywhere you want to go in the world, and once you get there, you can do whatever you want. You will still face some challenges (this is what we call *turbulence*), and you will have to figure out how to deal with certain issues. It also talks about using the 7 spirits of God to speak to a broader audience in the areas of wisdom, understanding, knowledge, counsel, might, and fear of your creator, all leading into the spirit of your creator, as the undeniable force of love to conquer evil in this world. After becoming a minister, I did a sermon on Isaiah Chapter 11, explaining the significance of the 7 spirits as the root of Jesse and the branch of King David, as the characteristics of Jesus Christ. As 7 is a number of completion, it is imperative that we seek a whole life as a complete person in this world. This book will not make you a complete person but serves as a roadmap to point you in the right direction for self-completion and mastery over the things you can control in your life.

The 7 navigators are the 7 guiding forces that aids you in your progression of life. There are things in this world that we must become more aware of. We detail these forces as wisdom, understanding, council, might, knowledge, and the fear of your creator, which leads to the spirit of your creator. These seven forces will give you the necessary tools and lessons that you need in order to take your life to the next level.

These forces allow you to live a complete life. It only takes you 7 years to reinvent yourself, and then you can realize that there are a lot of things that can help you in your journey. You will be able to learn how to acquire new skills in your life. We all have a thing called a *true north star*. This is the idea that we can all gravitate toward our life's purpose. As the journey of life sometimes takes us off our paths, we can look to the *true north star* to always lead us back to our destination. In our daily life decisions, we must understand that there will be things that will lead us on our paths, and things that will lead us away from our paths. But as we become aware of what we do, we can start making decisions that will lead us on that path. As we spiritually evolve, the *true north star* lead us not to a destination, but the progression of a worthwhile life goal.

Where to Begin?

It just starts with being curious. I would have to tell you that if you want to figure out where you need to go, you must start asking yourself why you want the things that you desire. Write down what you want to accomplish and when you want it. Think about where you want to begin, because it all starts with the things that you have in your possession, going beyond material things, because you may not be able to bring material things with you on your journey. A part of your preflight checklist is to figure out your talents and your passion, and once you figure those two things out, then you will know what activities you can put yourself into, to be able to develop your talents and your passion. Through those activities, in the form of schoolwork, an extracurricular activity, or an additional duty at your workplace, there will be an opportunity to meet people or do things that align with your talent and your passion; and at this point, it is important to find the people that share those same talents and passions, so that you can align yourself with better quality people at every level as you go up higher. When you immerse yourself in your talents and passions, then you will find that certain opportunities come out of your activities.

Because there is always someone watching you, you must be aware of the implications of your actions to other people. My first opportunity as a writer came in the form of a poetry contest, at Cameron Elementary School, in San Antonio, Texas. After writing a poem about my mother, I won first place in the contest and was invited to recite the poem in front of a crowd of 200 people, at an award show, at the end of the semester. After receiving praise and admiration from my teachers and classmates, I started to realize that I have an interest in writing. It wasn't until high school that I started to invest myself back into my writing, through my literature courses and reading *The Odyssey*, by Homer. I started to understand that the poetry within literature was able to speak to me through the pages of the book, and it gave me a thrill that was better than winning in sports or music. I was able to visualize myself in the book, and I remembered that my passion for poetry was able to give me the interest that I needed in order to hone my skills in writing.

Every journey has a period of self-discovery, and a point where you have no idea where to start. This is the moment where you must find your internal compass. In life, we are always given tools that don't look like what they appear to be—things that seem outside of our comfort zone.

As a pilot, you will not be able to take off without a qualified list of activities that you must do before even leaving the terminal to hit the runway. The idea for you is to be aware of the 5 things that we must all possess to be able to embark on any journey. Taking off without completing everything on your checklist can prove fatal, as life is a game of detail.

You must always remember to use your gift before it is too late—before life puts you into a corner, and fear keeps you there. But there will come a point where you will have to ask yourself: "When will enough be enough?" You have certain talents and abilities that the world must see, and when you leave this earth, you don't want people asking, "What could that person have written, sung, or done to make this world a better place?"

1. What do you want to be when you grow up?

This involves a question of vision. As children, we all had 1 or more occupations that we wanted to have. Once you remember that first sign of who you wanted to be, it will give you somewhere to investigate, on the path you will need to take. When I was 10 years old, I always wanted to become a teacher. As I grew older, I changed my decision because I only thought of teaching in a classroom. A few years ago, I learned that my childhood dream could take me to places beyond the classroom, but I had to learn to not make money my motivation, and to allow my heart's desire to drive me to my own definition of happiness.

2. What are your strengths?

A few questions I asked myself while growing up: What were my favorite classes? What comes easy to me while others must work hard for the same result? What can I throw myself into that makes the time pass quickly? Becoming aware of your skills and talents gives you the first sign of the path you must take to grow into the person you are destined to be. Life is a continuous process of self-awareness, and as you grow through the seasons of your life, your goals and desires may change, but your natural born skills will give you more direction on what will bring you happiness.

3. Who is in your support system?

A simple concept that many people take for granted is that the collection of people who are looking after your well-being will be crucial. Friends and/or family will give you a network of emotional support as you begin your journey. If you are blessed enough to have 1 or more people who give you guidance and direction, be grateful for the love they give, and remember that people will be there for you, even if they may not understand you. Life will sometimes get uncertain for all of us; and it is at these moments when you realize that plans fall apart and decisions change at the drop of a hat, and you will find out the people you surround yourself with will either lift you up or pull you down.

4. Where do you want to go?

Our society has taught us to guide our life toward credentials (job, degrees, etc.) and not purpose. By allowing yourself to think about where you want to take your life, the answers you seek will come in opportunities or people you meet. In the book, *Think and Grow Rich*, Napoleon Hill explains how "thoughts are things," the idea of what consumes your mind will come out in what you see in the physical world. As you grow to become aware of the power of your mind, you will learn that you in fact control the things that come to you, the more you think on a thought. Life can sometimes be unpredictable and unfair, but it will depend on how you react to your coming challenges, so that you will be able to develop your inner strength to handle the pressure of achieving your greatest goals and dreams.

5. Who to listen to

Looking at the example my father provided, my family made it a priority to place me on the proper path to gain an education and a well-paying job. I have realized as I seek to gain cruising altitude, it will be up to me to fly the plane and not allow others to fly the plane for me. I have lived my life for others and not myself, a common mistake other people share, living out others' dreams and not their own. This path of life can lead to unfulfillment and emptiness, even after a lifetime of achievement and excellence. It is important for you to remember what your true heart's desire is, and look to the people who support you, regardless of the path you choose. A true role model can come from anywhere, to where you are, because the true mark of wisdom will take humility to look to others who have been where you want to go and follow them. Growing up, I looked to my grandfather as my first role model. He was a father of 5 and a loving husband, and the first black architect in San Antonio. It took a great deal of maturity to realize that I could take the best of him and leave the worst of him behind, a lesson I had to learn on my own. Allow yourself to be open-minded, and ask for guidance from teachers, coaches, friends, and mentors to gain insight on your faults and ideas of how to progress yourself in your studies or occupation.

"Not every brother is your friend, and not every friend is your brother," is a quote that has allowed me to discover the true intent of others throughout my life. Knowing the difference between advice for your best intent, and the best intent for them, will give you insight on what will lift you up or let you down. The idea you want to think about, when you're trying to figure out who to listen to, is whether this person or this advice is getting you closer to your goal or getting you away from your goal. When you ask somebody a specific question about anything, is this person giving you the best advice for *your* intent, or for *their* intent? This is where you must truly depend on your true support system to be able to give you the needed wisdom that you need so you can go off and do the right thing. There was a time when I felt like I couldn't listen to anyone because I didn't know who I could trust, and I had to look back and remember that my true support system was only made up of five people—my mother, brother, uncle, grandfather, and my best friend. Because I knew that there was no motive behind the wisdom that they gave me, whatever they told me, I knew they wanted the best for me. It may have been something that I didn't want to hear, but it was advice that I needed in order to be able to move forward, regardless of how I felt about them or the situation. I knew for a fact that whatever they told me, I could believe in them because they believed in me.

An Additional Note: Pallbearers and Stretcher Bearers

A pallbearer is seen to carry someone as they leave this world, having a deep connection to the one who has passed on. In a practical context, you can think of a pallbearer carrying someone to their grave in the form of your words and actions, taking others closer to their death. A stretcher bearer is someone that carries you to life, to healing or support. You may never personally know who your stretcher bearer is until you come face to face with them, but it can also be said that your biggest supporters may be strangers. As we continue in our lives, it is important for us to be givers of life through our words and actions, to help your brother or sister in need. If you seek to rise to a higher level in life, it is important to remember that you will need the support of others, and their acts of support may not come until you show the same level of support first. Although you may never be perfect in your acts of kindness and loving others openly, it is your will to follow your conscience, and give yourself to others when they need you the most.

Reading Between the Lines: A Seed

A small idea, a spark of inspiration, or a word of wisdom, which makes us think deeper about what is possible to come out of the moment, can be the seed that is planted in our minds to change the direction of our lives. Imagine yourself as a gardener, tending to the seeds you plant in others to help them to see their own potential and self-realization. It will be up to the Universe to water the seeds that you deliver, so be confident in the fact that you will manifest your dreams by allowing yourself to be a vessel of love, giving yourself away to others in your daily life, and becoming an example that others can look to for inspiration or guidance. Everything in this world has a humble beginning. You are like a plant in the soil; you need time to turn into something that will grow out of even the worst conditions. But we must understand that the best things in life take time to grow from the soil, and we must understand that a small idea that we possess in our lives will take time to be able to grow.

A question that you can ask yourself is, what are you willing to invest your time into? Are you willing to put in the work so that you can see a reward? It is important to play the long game in life, to be able to learn how to venture into something now in order to receive a reward much later in life. A story I usually reflect upon is the Chinese bamboo tree, which is a rooted plant that takes up to five years to grow with constant water and care. But after a span of 5–6 weeks, it grows up to 90 feet. Even the greatest things in life take time, and you must be able to understand that when you overextend yourself, you are not giving yourself the needed time to grow in the areas you desire. Commit yourself to just two or three priorities, and then you can have the needed time for each priority, and you will be able to see the results of your progress, day in and day out.

Even the greatest trees started as a seed in the darkest of soil. In your journey, realize that your dark times will provide the strength to learn from your challenges. Everyone will undergo what I call "a great life struggle"—a test that will challenge you mentally, physically, and spiritually. Take solace in the idea that the Universe never intended to destroy you, but it will equip you with the necessary tools to take on greater challenges in the future.

Chapter 2

Understanding

*"I believe in living today.
Not in yesterday, nor in tomorrow."*
– Loretta Young

Experience

The first step in understanding someone else's vision and dream is to live the experience through your own eyes. It is only through your own experiences that you will be able to understand the true meaning of a life that's lived in another person's shoes. Because once you're able to understand the true picture and the reason why people make the choices that they do, then you will have the full picture of the decisions that you have to make, and of the things that you may have to do, based on the choices that you have before you. The thing about experience is that you can't gain it through any material possession; you must live it, and the only way to live experiences that can speak to other people is to go through your own set of trials and challenges. I believe everyone has a great struggle in their lifetime. This is where a test of your heart, soul, and character will bring out the best in you, or it will bring out the worst in you, as you try to move to the next level. It is with this experience that you will learn your life's greatest lessons, the people that you need to stick with, and your main priorities that you will have to stand by. Never would I have imagined that in order to reach the level of achievement in my life, I would have to choose between gas money and food during my journey.

During college, when I faced my lowest point, I had to decide what was important to me before I could decide what was important for anyone else in my life. It was the spring semester, in 2012, when I was still looking for a job, and I had to figure out what I was going to do with the allowance that my mom gave me for food and gas money. But due to my spending habits, I always threw money away buying unnecessary food and drinks for parties with friends, which put me in a bad spot. I would ask her for money, having few answers as to where it was going. It had gotten to the point where she refused to send me any more money for the next week, so I had to figure out how to make ends meet between my rent payments, the light bill, food, and gas. With only $10 in my checking account, I used $5 to purchase a can of cream of mushroom soup, bread, water, and ramen noodles. And I used the other $5 for gas for the next three days.

I eventually learned how to prioritize my spending, but I had to go through the experience of having little to no support, to show me the value of surviving with the little money I had. If it wasn't for that experience, I would not have learned the true value of surviving on my own,

Understanding

because I would not have a concept of true survival without the security of my family supporting me. This is the lesson that a lot of people will never learn, because they always have a safety net to fall back on, which can prove to be fatal based on the challenges that one will face. But through that experience, I learned I had more within me than I thought I had before. The true strength in your character will be called forth when you face your toughest challenges, but you must experience the true struggles of life in order to see what you are truly made of. Experience the strange teacher that will never tell you when the test begins, but it will always let you know when the test ends, and it will be up to you to determine what choices you will have to make, based on where you are in your life.

It is important to note that before you judge others, be sure to know the experience that they have had with the choices that they make in their lives, because once you understand the context of their decisions, then you would be able to see what they see, and feel how they feel. This is the beginning of having empathy with other people, so that you will be able to figure out how to respond to the choice that they make when it affects you. So, it will be important that you respond based on the experience they have had, so that you can understand both your experience and their experience, and it will prove to be the common bond that will bridge your relationship. Experience can be a harsh teacher and a good master to others, but the idea is that we all share the experience of being alive and present in the moment. When you figure out how your experience can be like others' experiences around you, even with different backgrounds, cultures, and nationalities, then you can truly figure out how to match your experience with the experience of others around the world. We all share this existence, and this existence is something that we are all given to make the most out of, but it will be lived out and experienced by all of us.

Judgment

Judgment can be something that causes us to have a prejudice against other people. It can be seen in an unsuspecting way, and brings out the worst in us. When we judge others, it shows a reflection of our true selves, and is why we compare ourselves to other people. It is the thing that will keep us from connecting with another person, because there is a hidden motivation that separates races, nationalities, and ideologies from coming together and finding a way to coexist in this world. The thing about judgment is that it is given too excessively and is never withheld from another's discretion. There will come a point in time when you have to be able to decide whether you will have to judge others based on what you see about them, or judge yourself based on what you see in the mirror, because the biggest judgment that we usually give ourselves is the judgment of our own iniquities. We usually judge others based on the fear of that person being a threat to either our existence or our own opportunities. But we must learn the lesson and not fear others, and we must evaluate the bias that we have for people that are different from us. All my life, I have seen myself judging because they do not possess the same ambition and drive as I have, but for two years I had to learn that through judging other people, I am actually separating myself from connecting

Understanding

with somebody that can teach me something. True wisdom comes from opening yourself up to be able to sit with like-minded people, and not allow your prejudices to get in the way of that person's character and personality. There will be too many opportunities that are lost when you judge yourself as superior to anyone else, because you never know who can teach you something, no matter their place in life. There will come a time in your life when others will judge you based on unreasonable circumstances, and at that point, you will have to figure out whether to treat others in the same manner or stop the cycle. It is up to you, and only you, to change the way you respond to others' criticism about yourself, and you can decide whether to allow judgment to damage you mentally, or use it as an alluring experience, where you can show others the same empathy that others have shown you. In my studies, I have seen the places where my unfair judgment of others can take me, and it leaves me alone and leaves me in a place where it isolates me from the crowd. While it is important to sometimes separate yourself from the masses, unfair judgments can put you in a place where you are susceptible to depression and mental trauma. The important thing to note is that when you feel the need to compare yourself to others, there is no comparison. Your journey and another person's journey are two separate paths, and when you realize the fact that every person has a unique journey to live out, and that your skills and talents are different from another person skills and talents, then you will be able to achieve self-mastery, and understand the fact that true judgment is not in another person but within yourself and who you were yesterday.

It is said that in order to love others, you must first love yourself. By unfairly judging yourself harshly, you are allowing yourself to be put in a place of mental chaos. Do you think about all the experiences that you have had, and compare yourself to others, and create a trail of psychological stress within your life that will always lead up to a breaking point? It can show us the most depressing path that comes from the choices that we make in how we treat others, creating a slippery slope for us, as life will seem to suffocate us based on the hatred that we have for others. It can consume us and can bring us closer to our destruction, because it puts us in a negative place that we may not get out of in our lifetime. As a result, we must use our power of judgment to be able to decide what opportunities and what people will give us the much-needed lift in our spiritual journeys, our careers, and in our relationships.

An Epiphany

On your journey, the greatest actions come to life when you receive a spark of imagination. A small idea to be built into a massive vision is the starting point of what we call an epiphany. An epiphany is a small realization and response, giving you a hint of what is to manifest based on your actions and your words as implied in that direction. Become a believer in your beliefs, which will have to become a conviction in which you are willing to take action to make your epiphany come to life. The power of thought cannot be overstated here, because based on your subconscious mind, you have been given certain thoughts in a flash of brilliance for a split second to show you what

Understanding

is possible outside of your environment.

The important thing to note is that you should always record your findings. As you walk through life, there will be times when you need to reflect back on the thoughts that were outside of your comfort zone, so that you will be able to figure out what is necessary to reach something that is outside of your comfort zone. During nighttime flights of an aircraft, there are two lights that illuminate on the tips of the wings to show ground control, as well as other airplanes in flight, of the vehicle that is approaching. The obvious question would be why it would be necessary for ground control to see a plane, when they can just track the plane on their GPS. The answer lies in the need to see the head of the aircraft in the physical space in order to guide it where it needs to go. In other words, it is necessary that you look at your physical, mental, and spiritual environment in order to figure out what steps you need to take to have your idea come to life. Your mind will show you what is possible, but only through intention can you properly navigate yourself to reach the destination with proper goal setting, guidance, and self-reflection. As a creative thinker, I share the same sentiments when a lot of ideas come through my mind, and I never record them, always wondering what thoughts are possible and what thoughts are lies to myself.

The reason why I didn't act on my awesome epiphanies in the past is because I didn't believe that I could attain them. I have come to find that the epiphanies only come through my own personal reflection and the experiences that I've had in my life, to show me what is possible when

I am willing to stretch myself outside of conventional means. The more that we are aware of the power of an epiphany, the faster we can adhere to the law of intention, stating, *"The quality of intention on the object of attention will orchestrate an infinity of space-time events to bring about the outcome intended."* This means that for us to create something out of ourselves within our lifetime, it is important to choose to give attention to a thought repeatedly in order for us to create the environment to meet the right people and opportunities, and to develop the skills necessary to accomplish our goals.

When you realize your potential in the ability to live off your epiphanies, then you can begin the process of being led by your subconscious mind in the true intention of where your life should go. You must learn that the Universe will speak through you in the form of other people, dreams, the media, and epiphanies. These forms of inspiration are the very first step in how we evolved as a species. Man's greatest achievement was the ability to process these forms of inspiration into physical manifestations of life. And as a result, we have the same power as the greatest minds of mankind, but it is up to us to tap into this power and realize that everyone is given an epiphany of thought, and the resources to make it come true.

What is Your Vision?

Most people that live on Earth do not have a clue as to where they're going within the next 5, 10, or 15 years. It is only a select few that can think of where they would like to go as a long-term goal. For you to properly navigate

Understanding

through the challenges of life, it is important to become aware of your *true north star*. As a symbol in your life that directs you on the path to your success when you are trying to achieve a goal, you must remain focused on where you are going. In this instance, your *true north star* serves as a long-term vision for yourself and your family as well. Your vision is your prized possession of all the accomplishments of your life, because it declares that you are purposeful in your direction and how you will get there. It is important to know that you can change based on the circumstances of your life, but it is also imperative that you hold fast to a vision to be able to evaluate your life after a certain amount of time.

Think about your long-term goals and the things that you are most passionate about. It is important not to allow material possessions to drive your vision, and to shape your vision for the benefit of others, because as you lose yourself in the service of other people, then you will be able to establish a vision that is greater than yourself. But when you shape your vision based on a material goal or on your own self-promotion, you can limit yourself as to how big your vision can grow, because it is not outside of yourself. When you understand the fact that a true vision is outside of yourself, and that it involves families, cultures, and communities, then you will be able to figure out how your vision will feed into the ultimate tapestry of the universe. At this point in my life, I feel like my vision is constantly evolving with the more information I learn, and the further out I reach goals around the world. One of the hardest things I had to do in my life was to find my personal potential through my purpose, and what the true vision for my life was and where I was going. Figuring out why you are here on this Earth is the greatest question of them all, but the tools necessary to find your purpose would involve you setting out for a long term, allowing life to adjust it accordingly. As you mature and connect with more people, your vision may change, as plans sometime do. Once you can define your vision for the world to see, then your decisions become simple. People and priorities that were at the top of your list before, will have to be evaluated to make sure that they align with the vision that's in your mind. It is always a tough decision to be able to choose the right path and the right people on your journey, but in order for you to grow, it will be important that you allow your own intuition and self-guiding system to place you in the right moment at the right time.

The hard decision that we must make as people is to seek our vision or stay on the sidelines and watch life pass us by. But the rewards of seeking your vision will outweigh the regret of watching your dreams and goals fall by the wayside. The weight of regret is so great that most people do not live to see the end of their lives because of the guilt that is within them for not taking the chance and being the person that the Universe called them to be. The greatest injustice that we can commit is by not allowing ourselves to be able to go out and be the people that we were supposed to be. It is okay not to have your vision figured out at this moment, but the most important thing you can do for yourself is to think critically where you would like to be in the next 5 to 10 years. When you figure out the answer of where you would like to be, then you must work back to figure out how to get there. And from there, you will be able to figure out the true path that you were meant to be on.

Faith and Strategy

In your journey, faith will serve to be a guiding force for you in your life. When you think about the true definition of faith, it involves the belief in things that are unseen. This is not to be confused with religion or rituals, but it is something to manifest for you and your life through your belief and what is possible for you to accomplish. For you to be able to use most of the power of faith, you will need to place yourself in uncomfortable positions, where there is nothing left to do but to believe that the unseen will appear in your life. For most people, this can be very difficult because it involves them doing things that are not their strong suits. It is important to know that faith is like a muscle that needs to be exercised for it to be more effective in your life.

You need to live your life expecting a blessing instead of begging for a blessing. There were numerous times in my life where I saw faith in such an uncomfortable experience, and I didn't understand what it meant to believe in the unseen. It wasn't until high school that I started to see the fruits of my labor based on the work that I put into sports, school, and music. At that point, I realized that if you invest your time into doing something productive in your life, then you can have an opportunity that will come out of the work that you do today. It is important to note that a strategy will need to be laid out in order to develop your vision and faith. This is the activator that will allow you to stay focused on your strategy during the grind of daily life. The way that faith and strategy work together is to combine the spiritual and the realistic perspective of the world, giving you an opportunity to lay the foundation while still looking ahead to the future. The steps you can do to combine your faith with your strategy is to set a goal that is outside of your control, whether it's a weekly goal, monthly goal, or a yearly goal. Create an action for yourself that involves someone else, so then you can see the power of thought and action as it aligns itself with your true intentions within your strategy. That is the essence of faith, that you are able to accomplish your goals that are outside of your control, but it will be up to you to set the goals in motion by putting intentions behind your actions, with the skills that you develop and the positions that you put yourself into, to be at the right place at the right time.

There will be a time in your life where you won't be able to depend on your natural talents to get you where you need to go, and you will need assistance from the Universe to show you the way when you start losing focus and need to depend on discipline to carry you to the next level. If you can have enough faith in the daily practice of habit, you will be able to understand the power of a long-term goal to keep you on the path that you seek. It is important to remember that faith without works is dead, and that you will need to be able to set up a daily goal list, with your daily thoughts, in order to consume your mind with an accomplishment, and then to detach yourself from the result. The result that you were looking for will be different from the goal that you seek, because the process of achieving a goal might go beyond the result that you were looking for in the beginning. The process is what we seek to get us to where we want to go, in a different place in life, and we understand the fact that whatever the process is that we subject ourselves to, is the point of our existence.

Peaks in the Valley

Before my exaggerated financial crisis at Prairie View, I faced a previous setback that placed me in a position of scarcity early on in my life after high school. I was enrolled at Virginia Polytechnic Institute and State University where I spent 2 years as an engineer major before dropping out due to academic performance. My family lived in Virginia at the time, and due to a layoff, had to move back to Texas. I spent a semester back in my hometown doing nothing, dangerously drifting away from the values and beliefs my family taught me. I remember multiple arguments with my mother, as she would physically will me to get out of bed. Soon I was eventually kicked out of the house for a few days, looking to my friends for sanctuary. It was at that point where I acknowledged I had to develop a focused plan to get back on track and re-write the story before it ends. When looking back on this experience, I consider this moment to be a valley in the early part of my life, as I was in my most desperate hour, wondering how low I would have to go to find food or additional money in case of emergency. There was a silver lining in that ordeal that came to mind looking back, showing my resilience to remain honest in any situation. When others would resort to violence or crime just to survive, I had the belief that God would ensure my well-being and safety if I upheld my moral obligation of righteousness.

There is no one in this existence that is guaranteed an *easy life*. The challenges that we all face may differ, but the Universe will test us on our level of moral endurance to see if we will be a value or a hindrance to the world. There will always be those who possess material wealth in this world and will be morally destitute, begging the question, "How can someone so evil have so much wealth?" But I would argue that the wealth you seek, material or spiritual, is within your reach. The challenge that you may not see is a journey of quiet desperation for others. An identity crisis is a common problem the wealthy elite face in this country, in using material gain to solve emotional or psychological problems that working class or poor citizens are not aware of. The stories we don't hear in the daily media cycle involve the deeper issues that we face on a larger scale, ironically destroying the fabric of this world. Communication is the key in order to lift you from your lowest experiences in life, to find your true treasure in your darkest hour. The pain and suffering that my uncle, Bernard Hartfield, faced since childhood is a prime example of how a lifetime of sickness and pain gave him the endurance to remain resilient and hopeful. He spent most of his youth in walking braces to gain the strength to walk. During his high school years, he was paralyzed for 3 years as he worked to gain the strength to walk again. Not knowing if he would ever walk again, he was forced to remain optimistic as my grandmother would pray for him and encourage him to remain in physical therapy until "God made a way for him." When remembering his experience, he said, "Everything else in life is nothing if I can handle this."

Understanding

The darkest times will never be pleasant for us, always adding stress and heartache that some never live through. My dear reader, I will never have the perfect words to tell you of how to overcome your personal battles in any situation. What I can tell you is that there will always be a lesson and a new level of emotional intelligence you will possess once you are on the other side of your personal struggle. As you pray for comfort and guidance in your journey, remember that you have been placed in a special time and place in order to become a better version of yourself; and that you are equipped to handle all situations with the proper resources and skills necessary to be successful.

In the next chapter, we will cover the proper tools for uncovering your hidden skills and areas of growth, in order keep you on track as you make your ascent after takeoff.

Chapter 3

Counsel

*"If I have seen further than others,
it is by standing upon the shoulders of giants."*
– Isaac Newton

Call For Help

During the time when I flunked out of Virginia Tech and started attending Prairie View A&M, I faced an identity crisis that I am discovering more about to this day. Just like other men in this world that face failure on the dreams they thought were right for them, I was angry at myself and the world for not being good enough to finish what I started, and I was questioning my worth as a man. Because of this frustration, I would isolate myself from my friends and family, contemplating throwing it all away and leaving the country and starting over. I had no idea of how to cope with the depression that came out of my failure but to turn to sex and drugs, to escape from my reality while working to get my degree and digging myself out the mental hole I had dug myself into. Once proving to myself that I was able to graduate with the engineering degree I sought, and to validate my intelligence, I developed a dismissive attitude toward people who were against my ideas and way of thinking. This caused me to lose a lot of friends and associates during my undergraduate years and the first 2 years in the Airforce, giving me cause for concern. When I acknowledged the fact that I showed a pattern of destructive behavior toward others, I was ready to seek mental therapy to discover what triggers this behavior and find ways to maintain healthy relationships.

Pride can be a defense mechanism to protect our self-image as we seek a sense of belonging among our peers during each season of our life. If left unaware, it can distance us from others as we create personal narratives as the victim and not the culprit. Once you can accept the idea that everyone in this world develops an imbalance during some point in their lives, then you can be ready to address the mental and emotional imbalances from your past. Life is a journey of self-awareness that uncovers the darkest parts of our personalities, and the pain we give to others reflects the hurt in our hearts for a person, experience, or emotion we are lacking.

We must change the stories we teach our youth in how to handle the stress and anger that accumulates over years of misinformation. Meditation and counseling are a testament of mental strength to face the darkest parts of the mind in order to uncover the cause of irregular behavior in schools and workplaces. A call for help starts from within, and it takes an incredible amount of confidence to speak to a professional about what is needed. There will come a time when we start to notice a pattern forming in our

Counsel

relationships and how they end. For some people, it takes a lifetime to discover that we are responsible for the people we attract in our lives, and how we interact with them. But if you choose to take the barren path and uncover the emotional triggers that repel you away from the people that you love the most, you will be rewarded with clarity of who you truly are, and you will be given the awareness about yourself to allow love back into your life, in spite of the pain that life brings to all of us. When embarking on your journey for mental and emotional intelligence, this navigator will prove to thrust you in the face of your darkest secrets, and show you what will be required to harness this force to benefit you. But before we can develop a strategy in facing these demons, there are tools that will be necessary to obtain the courage and support to conquer what may be the greatest struggle within your life.

True Connections

The people that matter most to you and your life will not always be family or friends. True connections come from anyone that you come across in life, and the people that you surround yourself will determine a lot about your destiny. It goes deeper than those you have things in common with; it goes to another level where people in your life sacrifice themselves for you, so you can do the same for them. When your most desperate hour of need comes, these will be the people that will come to your aid at the drop of a hat. There must be an understanding of the true family in your life that you share so many connections with.

Sometimes the people that you least expect to be your greatest advocates, will be strangers. Although you may be on a different path than everyone else, there are people that share the same morals and ideals as yourself, and that is where your true connection begins. When you align yourself with people who believe in the same things as you, the world is a vast array of ideas and cultures, and the object isn't to sway people to your way of thinking but to find the ones that already think on your wavelength. How many times have we questioned a person's loyalty based on the way that they treat us? We must understand that the idea of loving others starts with ourselves, and that we can't base another person's connection on how much we love them, but we must base a true connection on how much we love ourselves when we are around these people. Do they allow us to be our true selves? Do we feel joy and happiness whenever we come in their presence? These questions are needed to be answered before we decide to spend a significant amount of time around the people in our lives, because without self-fulfillment, we become lost in our emotions.

It is time to face the fact that when we are around others, we must make the decision to be able to let them go or to embrace them based on how we feel around them. So many times, we suffer in toxic relationships because we are afraid to let go of the person that claims to love us. Even though they abuse us and manipulate us, we somehow feel a need to stay connected because we forget how it feels to be alone. But the fact is, it is best when we can enjoy our own company, and then once we are content to be on our own life journey by ourselves, then we will be

Counsel

able to embrace another life within our existence. There must be a period in order to be able to learn the tools necessary to nurture and care for another person.

When I think about a true connection, I think about my brother and my sister-in-law, and the example of their marriage as a perfect balance of love and teamwork. Tim and Toni share the same morals, which they have passed down to their children. Both have the fear of their creator in their hearts, and were able to work through their relationship issues, and work on their relationship to a level of mutual respect always. This form of communication should become a law for our society, that when two people come together, communication must be critical for them going forward, to get past their differences and to remind themselves of the true nature of their love for each other. As we dive deeper into the power of counsel, it is necessary to understand that only with true connections are you able to give your full emotions to love another person, and these people have to be accepting of your ideas, and be non-judgmental of the way you think, because there will be times when you will be afraid to see who you truly are, and those are the people that you will need to encourage you to face your fear of yourself, and learn how to cope with your deepest and darkest issues.

The Counselor

Your counselor is a conduit for your thoughts to manifest out into the world for third-party application. As you imagine this person that is leading you on your journey, you will be able to remember that your counselor is sacrificing their time to ensure that your life is in order. There is no greater responsibility in this world than to be accountable for somebody else's life, and the person that you look to for this mentorship should be somebody that has accomplished what you aspire to have. The trials aren't to face your fears; they only begin when you have acknowledged that it's okay not to be okay.

I would like you to remember a person or group of people that has a significant influence in your life— someone who can speak to you in your time of need, when everyone else around you doesn't understand you. You don't have to seek professional help on your path, but as you work to see yourself and to discover your true flaws, you will need to find somebody that can objectively assess where you are, and can help you to cope with yourself as you go higher in life. Our greatest weakness is the one thing that is keeping us from our true potential, because if we knew who we truly were in this world, then we would be able to harness our wisdom and knowledge to be able to manifest a spiritual existence for us and those around us. When I started seeking counsel, I was on the road to redemption from my initial failures. The moment when I thought I was okay was when I showed the most signs of illness. I coped with my failure at Virginia Tech by drinking, smoking, and partying, which served as a coping mechanism to avoid the reality of facing my fear.

The trial within my crisis was not in my academic performance but in my inability to accept responsibility for my life. I have observed that my father shared the same characteristics as I did— to look for another way out of the

Counsel

reality that life had given us—but there was a situation where I had to run forever, or stand my ground to push through my fear. The Universe tends to create a system around you that designs your life based on the strength of your spirit. It allows you to accept the trials of your life at your choosing. But don't be fooled into thinking that the timeline of your life will not proceed without you. The Universe will work in spite of you, but in order to avoid unnecessary pain in your life, you must accept the path that you are on, and acknowledge that you have the power to change the trajectory of your life—but only if you accept the responsibility of giving yourself to another spirit, and allowing them to listen to your inner most turmoil.

As we all know, love creates pleasure and pain in the same breath, and we choose to inhale or exhale as we need to give energy to the feeling. As you love yourself more, you will learn to make yourself vulnerable to this counselor, but you will open your eyes to a bigger perspective of the world. When you find someone that truly listens to you and gives you direction without bias, you must be willing to give your all to the effort. If you choose to hold back now, all you're doing is robbing yourself of the pleasure of uncovering the treasure within you. If you have been gracious enough to pick up this book, then I would like to declare a prophecy over your life: You are expected to share your story with other people that have been chosen, out of a 1 in 100 trillion chance, to create a significance in your existence. You are meant to do something that is bigger than yourself, but as you unlock the power of love to figure out who you are, you will have to conquer the demon within to share your love with thousands of people, to multiply yourself throughout the nations. It is my wish that you unlock the key to your life and let this writing spark your imagination, to ask yourself the question in order to complete your pre-flight checklist. I pray that you find the person necessary to guide you through your darkest spaces.

The Greatest Enemy

In the history of the world, the greatest battles were fought not for material possessions but the desire for power and control over one's environment. The question to ask is, what would cause humans to desire power and dominion over their own species? In the beginning of time, it was a duality of good and evil that formed, not on morality but on the choices that humans could make. It is because of this that man's greatest enemy lies within himself. As the power of choice creates a rift in this world, people can choose to be a benefit to the world or to watch as others destroy it. The greatest enemy to spirituality is the void of hope, and the nonexistence of a person making a choice for the benefit of others. As hope is lost in a person's mind, fear becomes a part of a person's existence. It is a fear of death and poverty that exists in all the hearts and minds of people, and only when they decide to free their minds of these fears, can they conquer their enemy.

Your greatest enemy will not be in human form; it will not have different ideas than you, and it will not oppose the way that you live your life. Your greatest enemy lies in the mystery in this world, led by influences that are naturally negative, based on the mindset of fear. For you to avoid becoming this a product of this world, you must acknowledge the fact that you need direction; and this will be the first step of your learning. As you understand the fact that you will need to connect to your spiritual Source, you will have the explicit choice of deciding to connect with the Universe at large, to change your mindset of fear into a mindset of abundance. It takes no effort to think negatively, but it does take a small effort to change the way you perceive the world, and look for the good in everything, instead of the bad.

As you continue your journey, you will understand that the darkest times are manifested in fear, but as you choose to allow the fear to stay there, it does not have to spread to the story of you. The true solution to overcome your greatest enemy will lie in your desire to create a vision for yourself that is outside of yourself. As you look at your pre-flight checklist, it will be important to note that the questions that you ask yourself will create some more questions, but solutions will come, and they're based on your desire to know the true answers for yourself. My fear lies in my relationships with others, because the idea of my darkness, being judgmental toward others, is being brought to the light. As I continue to ask myself questions of my existence and how I'm supposed to be able to use my personal relationships to grow and evolve, I am faced with new challenges and questions about how I see my world and how I treat other people within the perception of my mind.

Your feelings may be different from mine, but we both share the same quality—we lack the true nature of love within our mental health. As your answers become more questions to ask yourself, this is where your counselor will be a person that can direct you to what questions to ask in order to give yourself the answers that you seek. It is very important to connect yourself spiritually with the systems that will be needed, for you to continue going in the direction that you are heading. Where meditation will open your mind to the challenges that you must face, consulting will lead you to knowing how to approach the challenges, to give you the result that you need. There is no easy answer to give you on how to conquer your true demons, but the hope for you is that you acknowledge that there are things to conquer in your life, and that you'll be given the tools necessary to strengthen your will and look at yourself in the mirror to see who you truly are.

Full Circle

The power of a circle has a unique role in geometry, as it represents 360 degrees, a diameter, and sometimes a perimeter. 180 degrees represents a turnaround in your life, whereas 360 degrees must represent a return to who you are. I didn't understand the consequences of my choices would come back to affect my current state of well-being, and I was learning the lesson—a lesson that I call *full circle*. It is the idea that your choices echo what's in your mind to remind you of who you used to be, or of the dimension of who you are meant to be. For most people, you can mention that this is your conscience, but it goes to a deeper level. Imagine if the voice in your head could speak to your past and future in the same moment—a moment in time where you could see life adjusting itself for you. If it were hard or difficult, you would be able to see the people that the universe places in front of you and know in that moment what's supposed to happen. You would be able to see the opportunities that you were given and realize that the day could be in no other logical way in order to receive that choice—a little something was guiding you on that path. The power of the universal, omnipotent, all-knowing energy gives you what you need if you open your eyes to it, and you become aware of how to look for it.

I remember the moment when I decided to join the military. In my junior year, it was a regular class day, in the fall semester of 2011, and as I looked on the bulletin board in the engineering building, I was shocked to see a sign that was posted, looking for engineers in my major of study. This sign led me to enlist in the military and become an officer, when only 2 years before I had one dominant thought: to turn my life around 180 degrees, and gain discipline in my daily life by joining the military. From a national pool of talent, I was selected, in the spring of 2013, to join the United States Air Force. In my full circle moment, when I saw the flyer on the bulletin board, I saw my future and my past; it was something that spoke to me, to take the opportunity and acknowledge that it was just for me. Your thoughts have the power to bring you moments such as those, and to give you the guidance and clarity that you need in order to accept things with your name on it. As we look back on the opportunities that this world had to offer, we must consider the thin thread that we walk on to have the things that we are grateful for today. Because you look back on your life, the things that you desired in beginning may never fulfill you, and then when you think about what you want to be when you grow up, that might have been the first inkling of the full circle coming into your life.

You keep moving forward, but you never fall off the cliff, because you are always meant to circle back to where you started, at a higher level. The universe gives us a strange lesson, taking us on our chosen path and reminding us of our beginnings and the people that we started with in the past, which we had to live with for our survival. For you to realize your full circle moment, is to remember the thoughts that dominated your mind naturally. What were the things that always came to mind when you were trying to get your life back in order? What was that one goal that you wanted for yourself that was a complete turnaround from what you would usually do? The moment something or someone was placed into your life, based on those dominant thoughts you had, was the moment in time that your mind began to make another lap in the timeline of your life. You somehow used your birthdays as a timer reflection of your past year, but I would submit to you that your reflection can happen any day, and that is something to be celebrated. A death, the birth of a child, or a marriage are the moments that change the direction of our lives, and in a split second, it sets in and hits you, and that is when the anniversary begins.

Just a Regular Person

When I had a full circle moment about the people in my life, it was the first time that I realized who my parents truly were. It was the moment that my mother revealed to me that one of the reasons why she married my father was to leave my grandmother's house. But in doing that, she would have been choosing to move back into the same house she grew up in after my grandmother passed away, and that's when I knew she made the best decision she could with her experiences and resources in her life. She would always tell me about what could have been if she had known about my father before marrying him, and what could have been if she had decided to join the military. If my mother's early part of her journey was for control, my father's path was more about validation. He had the need to belong somewhere after his brothers graduated from college and left him at home. He made the decision to leave his responsibilities, and in his mind, he made the best decision he could, based on who he was, and based on what he felt his sons needed at the time.

These decisions can have a damaging effect on society, and families within the society, but if we are not educated on what other decisions are available, we doom ourselves to live a life of misinformation. That is why it is important for us to seek out what we need to make us happy, and not depend on other people for control or validation. When you let go of the emotional need to depend on others for your joy, you can achieve a level of freedom that only a few in this world have the privilege of living. As I continue my path of life, I've come to understand that my mother and father were just regular people, making decisions to get them by. As their child, I didn't have a say in my upbringing, based on decisions that they made. All of us now realize that when giving false information, what happens for you and your family is that you live a life of quiet desperation, and all your children can do is watch as you are forced to make decisions, not knowing the big picture.

When you think about the people that have raised you in your life, I would suggest that you take an objective look at who they really are and forgive them if you had to live a hard life during your childhood. Whether you had a positive experience or a negative one, there are some things that we cannot control, but we must control how we perceive that experience. It is then that we can learn a true lesson from it, and appreciate the people that gave us the opportunity to learn it. Your parents weren't just there to teach you your first lessons during childhood; they should be your first examples in your adulthood, of the trials and challenges that life can offer, and to be open for mature conversation about what's at stake with your daily decisions.

It may take a whole lifetime to forgive your parents or guardians for any wrong they have done to you, but when that full circle moment comes, you need to be ready. When you are ready to emotionally detach yourself from those years of pain and heartache, you will be able to unlearn the mental programming that was placed within you. You will be able to turn your life around to take full accountability for your decisions, and not expect anyone to make your choices for you.

In the next chapter, we will learn how to use might to push through your decisions when you meet resistance from the Universe, as your true test of endurance. The lessons of self-abandonment and self-observation were service key guides for your source of strength to deal with your separation from your previous life and the introduction to your new life.

Chapter 4

Might

"I am deliberate and afraid of nothing."
– Audre Lorde

A Sense of Abandonment

On your path to find your true self, you will notice that the journey is a bit lonely. It is natural to feel a sense of self-abandonment when you have decided to win your mind back, and you will have to make decisions that are different from the masses of people. During your ascent, there will be moments where you feel weightless, and you will have the feeling of just taking off and allowing your body to get used to the pressure that is applied on your life from others around you, while you go higher and higher. There is no easy way to tell you that this path is not for everyone; there will be difficulties and moments of self-doubt, and times where you will want to quit and throw it all away. You can be confident in your abilities to find the answer, if you connect to your spiritual source and use your talents to the best of your abilities.

My sense of self-abandonment started when I went to college. I felt that I was misunderstood from the time I got to know everyone. This goes back to my failure at Virginia Tech, and my coming to PV as a second chance to redeem myself and get my education. During my time with everyone on campus, I looked back at the things I did that were offensive due to my frustration of where I was, and of not knowing the reasons for how I got there in my life, and I took it out on all of them, unintentionally.

Looking back and learning more about myself, my identity crisis stemmed from figuring out who I was and why I was there in the first place. I have always sought to challenge myself in every part of my life, and I personally had frustration with others that looked for a shortcut to earn the same right I worked for to become a part of the organization. I have realized that this way of thinking was wrong on my part, and that everyone has their own personal challenges inside and outside of the social college scene. I felt I did not have a choice in leaving, and at times I wanted to separate and re-group my thoughts. I believe, at the time, I was looking to fit in somewhere when I first came to PV, and realized that I was never meant to fit in but to be unique and to contribute in my own special way to all the organizations that I was a part of during college. When looking further into my life, I had to realize that this pattern existed long before I was aware of it. Now I use the same sense of abandonment to empower me to reach out to others that are going through the same thing emotionally, and to encourage others to stay the course because it is preparation for the future.

Might

Dear reader, you are beginning to embark on a journey that everyone cannot go with you on, but your impact will be too important for you to be weighed down by what you will face. Your role in this world is too important for you to go through life as a drifter and to be unaware of what affects you mentally. It may be a confirmation or realization for you, but either way, you are not alone in this world, and even though there may be few dreamers, there will always be more people to support you on your path. As humans, we are communal creatures, always looking for a sense of belonging and a tribe to become a part of, but what we never talked about is our beginning and end, and the power that we possess in entering and leaving this world alone. As we reflect on this, it gives you a chance to remember that your moments of greatest personal growth may happen when you are by yourself, while others will be there to support and facilitate the environment in which you grow. There will be a sense of fear that runs in your heart because it is a habit to always have others around. Isolation is dangerous, but the point is not to deny yourself human contact, but to have discernment over the people that you choose to associate with that are not aligned with your life's path. It will take some time to figure out who you truly are, and to know who you should spend the majority your time with. But in doing this self-observation, you give yourself more freedom to see the world as it is.

Self-Observation

One of the most important things you can do with your life is to meditate. The simple practice of looking within yourself, in silence, provides your mind and body an opportunity to synchronize and rest during stressful times during the day. By committing yourself to 5 to 10 minutes of focused breathing a day, it can provide you more clarity in how you process your daily activities. There is something special when you discover things about yourself that you didn't know existed. There is a moment in our lives when we shift from blaming others for all of our problems, and finally take responsibility for our actions and consequences; but before that moment can exist, we must be available and open-minded to allow teaching from our mentors, so that they can show us the blind spots that we must address in order to grow.

It is widely known that our greatest challenges exists in how we see others and the life situation we are in, so the idea of self-observation will involve accepting the gap you must fill between who you are and the life you desire to live. This dimension of might will signal the beginning of the strength you must develop in order to face a world that will be unwilling to hand you your dream. Think of it as a mental shift you will take when you decide that you will no longer allow the world to control how you think and act, and be willing to always ask yourself what you can change about yourself in order to pass the trials of your life. My experience in network marketing was eye-opening; it showed me my weaknesses in developing healthy relationships with prospective clients and acknowledging the fact that I was cold and transactional in sharing my business with them. I was confused at times as to why my business was not growing, when I felt I had the necessary social skills and business knowledge. I neglected to see how my childhood had a direct connection to how I associated with friends and peers in my adult life.

As I began to see the true face of my enemy, it laid in the fact that the love that I expected to receive was not reciprocated to me, and my disappointment in not having my expectations met gave me a false sense of rebelliousness to become the person who loved others first without waiting for anyone else to do the same for me. This lesson would not have come without those silent moments of wondering how I could see others, when I was failing to see that all the results of my past business failures were because of my failure to love others with no expectations.

As you desire to reach cruising altitude, there will be times when you will have to ask yourself the same questions in order to see your own shortcomings, and allow others to serve as your confirmation of what is necessary for you to do to make your dreams come true. A practical source of guidance that you can connect to may be in religion, spirituality, or science, to find a model for you to follow in order to see how you can allow love to direct your choices and disconnect from the fear of loss or failure. The world will teach you that mistakes are fatal, but you must push through this barrier and learn to observe and find the lesson in the broken relationships and trauma in your past life experiences, because there are no accidents in the world, and the Universe will tend to repeat your tests until you are ready to look within yourself for the answers. For the rest of our lives, we will always have the necessary tools and resources to find the person or opportunity to bring out the best version of ourselves, but the masses will live in fear and make excuses for being too busy to take the time to look. But as you already know, vision goes beyond your eyes. You will have to develop this sixth sense in order to see the bigger picture of how you can control the circumstances of your life, by starting with thinking about how you think of the world around you.

Courage

In Webster's dictionary, *courage* can be defined as *"mental or moral strength to venture, persevere, and withstand danger, fear, or difficulty."* This idea can mean different things for you, based on how you relate this definition to your life experiences. But the overall idea you can take from how to use courage in your life, will involve you taking a step to act, regardless of the fear you may feel. The negative forces of the world use the vehicle of fear to discourage you from doing things that are uncomfortable. But there is an age-old saying that fear is an illusion, and the concept of *false evidence appearing real*. Our subconscious mind does not have the ability to know what is real and what is fantasy, and as a result, we suffer from fabricated ideas and think that they can harm us. This is not a claim that we are immune to the true dangers of this world, but this is a statement saying that most of your ideas and fears will not come true.

Mark Twain is quoted as saying that only 10% of your fears become reality, and the other 90% are fluttering ideas in your mind. There was a true fear that I felt when I decided to leave the military and pursue a career in writing and public speaking. The idea of lack and homelessness consumed my mind as I wondered how I could make money without the safety net of a steady paycheck; but in December 2018, I met a woman that told me of her journey from Jalisco, Mexico to the United States as an illegal immigrant, and her struggle to raise 2 children and look for work in a foreign land with no resources. Her embodiment of courage gave me the assurance that the fabricated propaganda that we receive from the media is promoted to paralyze us in the idea that we are only capable of being employees in a corporate world. But my desire of entrepreneurship is too strong to deny the pursuit of my dreams any longer. Your deepest desires may not be in the form of business or self-development, but you must find the ideas that will drive you to live a courageous lifestyle and to see through the fear that the world will try to put upon you in your pursuit of happiness.

Courage only means the fact that you will step toward your fears; it is natural to be afraid of the unknown. Put your faith in the universe, and it will pay dividends for you if you take one action within that place of discomfort.

No matter your craft or occupation, the courage that you show today will be opposed by the people that you may love the most, because they might not understand why you are doing what you are doing. In fact, the courage that you show may not be physical or mental, but it will come as an emotional battle to you. You must prepare yourself for the disappointment that you might see in others that don't want to support you in your journey. I consider this idea as the *rubber band effect*: As you pull closer toward your dreams, it will create a tension between you and the people that you love the most, until the break happens. This is where most of your emotional pain will come from, because some people cope with the separation better than others, and this is the thing that we may fear the most. The fear of loss is something that will always drive us to stay in our comfort zones. We are afraid to lose the friends and family that meant a lot to us in our past, but we have to determine if they are truly the people that will love us and let go of the fact that we have to stay miserable in order to be happy. The myth that most people believe is that their best days are behind them, but you can give them reason to relive them every day. The message I would like you to understand is that your best days are in fact ahead of you, and the people that you share your future with may not be the ones you expect.

The Rubber Band

I was raised with the belief that you will never be forsaken if you follow the path of righteousness. For my morality, that was a challenging decision that I made during my college years. When I began my network marketing business, I started to see the possibilities that life has to offer, and the quality of people that I need to surround myself with in order to live the life I desired. I started making choices to align myself with self-development and entrepreneurship, and that meant I had to separate myself from my current circle of college associates. I remember, at my lowest point, I isolated myself away from everyone, for fear that I was going to be misunderstood. I would have to explain myself to everyone that did not understand my journey.

Might

Thinking back, the tension that was created was mostly what I imposed upon myself, and had little to do with others around me. It was as if I saw the man that I was supposed to be when I looked at the man that I was in that moment, and I could not separate one from the other. When my friends would see this, I remember that I would always receive a certain look, as though they did not know who I was, and I looked unfamiliar to them. I'll never forget that look because it shows me that I have yet to uncover the man that I'm supposed to be.

The tension was building during my years at PV, and I remember the exact moment that the rubber band broke. It was a few days before graduation, and I was driving back from Houston, reflecting on the journey that I've come through from my failure at Virginia Tech, and almost throwing my life away in San Antonio. I drove my gray Camry past the university drive entrance, and I yelled out, "I win," through the window of my car. The emotions that came out of that moment were from me telling world that I refused to become my own worst enemy and defeat myself. But during this process, I've lost a lot of friends, and I wonder what could have been if I did not allow the pressure that I put on myself to cause me to lash out at my friends and associates.

It is very important for us to remember that if you would like to go somewhere you haven't been before, you should surround yourself with people of higher quality, and believe what you believe in. But the thing that others don't tell you is that you will have to be okay with letting go of the people that you grow accustomed to knowing. The tension that is caused when you are separating yourself from non-believers will be easier for some than others. But a suggestion that I can give you today is to embrace the assistance of a professional therapist. This form of counseling will be able to guide you on how to have a difficult conversation with the people in your life, and cope with the fact that everyone may not be able to come with you as you ascend higher.

There are not many dreamers in this world to begin with, and the worst part about achieving your passions and dreams is that there will be less and less people to join you on your path. This is a mental gap that we all must cross, but you must determine if it is worth the effort and the sacrifices you must make. The worst part about rubber band breaking is that it signifies the death of a life previously lived, and it can hurt because you thought that your comfort zone would be enough. The beautiful thing about your rubber band breaking is that it gives you a new freedom to discover who you really are, and to find the people that love you for you. This will give you encouragement when you face failures in business, your occupation, or your craft. The day will come when everything that you work for will come to fruition, and the vindication that you seek will be one of the proudest moments in your life, because you were right about what you believed in all along.

Vindication

The word, *vindication*, reminds us of the confirmation of our beliefs. This is the Universe's way of proving to us

Might

that the struggle was worth it. The navigator of courage brings out the best in us, and shows us the good and the bad side of standing up for what we believe in. It can sometimes be bittersweet because it can show you who your true friends are, and who your enemies may be. Choose to get past your fears, and you will reach cruising altitude. This is the part of your journey that will validate all the pain and suffering that you have endured. And make no mistake about it; the feeling will be euphoric for you and your moment of victory, and then you will reflect on the sacrifice that you must make for this to become possible.

I remember my graduation day like it was yesterday; and I remember the emotions that I felt as I walked across the stage and saw my family there to support me, and the friends I used to have, watching me in disbelief. I chose this path of life because I believe that the world requires more leaders to make the hard decisions and to lift the world up, regardless of who is there to cheer you on, or who is there to stop you. As I walked out of the basketball gym, holding my degree in my hand and thinking about my future, I knew there were still problems in my mind that I had to address. It was a relationship that I had to rebuild, but the unique thing about life is that as time goes on, there will be a chance to renew the opportunities that were lost; but it's important to move forward with your dreams and visions, to influence and impact the people that need you. The righteous will always find a way to win in the face of evil, no matter how dire the situation may seem; but it will be up to good men and women such as us to stand firm and see our dreams come to fruition.

With the unknowns of your life, and when you are not sure of where to find the answers, it will be important to remember why you are doing all of this. The idea of finding a "why" will be paramount on your day of victory, because that may be the only thing you receive for your service to mankind. It can seem like a thankless job, something that no one will acknowledge you for, but you must believe that there are others out there just like you, fighting the same battles. How do you know when your day of victory is coming? It begins when you feel the need to quit, and you want to throw it all away at a moment's notice. It will come in that small whisper that tells you to keep going, while everyone around you will tell you that what you are doing is useless.

In order to live like most can't, you must do what most won't do. The most courageous people I know are not the ones in uniform; they are people that are trying to make a living for their families, in an environment that is built for their destruction. We may never get to a point in our lives where everything is okay, but we must strive to be at peace—mentally, spiritually, and emotionally. When you feel at peace with your decisions and the life that you chose to live, this is the day that you can celebrate, because most people won't get the chance to. Every victory that you gain, you can be confident in the fact that you are prepared to handle bigger battles, and your righteous spirit will be tested to live life at a higher level.

Looking back, things weren't clear for me, and the answers didn't come when I wanted them to, but as the years go by, I start to understand why I chose the path I did, based on where I want to go. So, you must trust yourself to know that the vindication isn't about being the best or getting revenge—it's deeper. It shows you your purpose in this world, and as you navigate through the gray area of life, your victory will come. If the Universe placed your dream in your mind, then it will give you the next step needed. When you pray, ask for wisdom and understanding, because these two things will keep your mind clear to look for a pattern in your life that you can follow to see the big picture.

Clarity

In my meditations, I see my breath feeling the darkness like a cool breeze gusting through the night sky. At that moment, everything stands still because my mind is at peace, and after about 10 minutes, I open my eyes. Sometimes I see what's in front of me, but sometimes I see the next step forward. How can we explain the answers that come when they do? When you have been looking for a solution to your problem this whole time, and it just comes in a split second, you must ask yourself, "Why?" Why did it come when it did? Why couldn't it have come sooner, when you wanted it to? It may be because you were not ready for the solution, or perhaps life wasn't ready for your answer. Looking back on the past 10 years of your life, I can imagine that you can pick the most important moments that changed your life forever: the times you may have been in danger or the times you had boundless joy. But the fact is that you understand the reason why you went through the challenges you did, to learn the lesson that you know now.

My grandfather was the most significant male role model I had in my life. He has seven brothers and sisters and used to pick cotton and drive a taxicab in the early 1920s. Growing up in San Antonio, Texas, he earned his certification in architecture, and he would build blueprints for buildings throughout the east side of San Antonio. As a man of enterprise, he invested in real estate through commercial property, as well as in raw land cattle and crops. In my mind, he achieved the perfect balance of being a family man and a businessman. But upon his death, there were still some questions I had in my mind as I grew older. The main question was why he had never taught me how to build assets. Perhaps I was too young and was not ready to learn the lessons he had to teach? Or perhaps it was his plan to teach me, but he passed away too soon? Either way, it became clear to me why a desire for business was put in me: He was laying the blueprint of how to maintain assets, before I even knew what business was about. And now it's time to reclaim my family's assets and teach our next generation how to keep them. Your moment of clarity may not be a lesson that was from your family. It may in fact be the reason why you went through a bad experience, or why you have certain talents that you consume your time with. But the fact of the matter is that your moment of clarity will not come just by looking backwards; it will also come as you seek within yourself for the answers.

The greatest question that you can ask yourself is, "What do I need to change about me?" Your relationships, your lifestyle, and your purpose will depend on you seeking answers, and you don't know in which direction to go.

Things become clear for people at different times in their lives, and the moment comes spiritually, mentally, physically, and emotionally. These four moments may not be remembered in your dying days, but they are pivotal for you to appreciate what you had to go through in each phase of life. When you take that first step in courage, to see what to change about yourself, the moment of clarity feels so much sweeter. Now you know how to push further and reach higher to live the life that you desire. This moment, when everything comes to you, will depend on the accumulation of knowledge that you attain on your journey.

In the next chapter, we learn about our fifth navigator, which is knowledge, and how the pursuit of learning about the world and about yourself will guard you against your worst enemies. It is imperative to remember that the more knowledge you gain, the more responsibility you must give to others. And as you get into the daily practice of sharing your knowledge with other people, then you will realize that the world works in abundance and not in lack, and there is enough for everyone to reach their life's goals.

Chapter 5

Knowledge

"Wonder rather than doubt is the root of all knowledge."
– Abraham Joshua Heschel

A Lifetime of Learning

It is said that the average American only reads one book per year, which limits their perspective of the outside world beyond media. This could be one of the reasons that is tied to the miseducation of Americans and their public knowledge of world relations, because we know freedom not as a privilege but sometimes as a burden, and the more confused everyone is, the more that corruption can take a hold of our societies around the world. The greatest leaders throughout history have been voracious readers, meaning that their desire to learn information rapidly has been a contributing factor in their rise to power. In other words, *readers are leaders*, and in order to take a hold of your life, you will have to accept the common practice of learning information daily. This is your first step in the navigator of knowledge: to find a field that you take an obsessive interest in and seek to become the subject matter expert in it. As the world changes, information will rapidly change with it, and it is not enough just to read about your subject; let's create new ideas within it and start with the aspiration for knowledge.

When I learned that I had a talent for public speaking, I made it a point to learn everything I could about the business, and how to improve within my craft. I came to find out that public speaking is simple to do but has unlimited ways to effectively deliver what you want. Your audience always changes, so your delivery will always change. You should first ask yourself what you love to study, in or out of school. Looking back at this time, you could begin to see where your mind took you to another place, when you started to dig into your favorite subject. To become a student of your craft means that you must dedicate 10,000 hours. To become a master on the subject, to accomplish this great task, you must find something that turns you on. You will begin to feel a labor of love to help not just yourself but other people who want the same thing that you do.

People usually stop learning when they stop going to school, but the end of school only signifies the beginning of learning; it means that you already have the skills to become productive in the field you choose. My initial failure in business was a lesson in obsession, because of my pursuit of business knowledge and then failure. Looking back, I can see the skills that I attained based on my dedication to learn everything I could. And now I see my failure as a learning experience, because it equipped me with the tools necessary to bet on myself and take my life

Knowledge

to the next level. When you pick a path, you must focus and sell out to the challenge in front of you, because the value of dedicating yourself to one thing will give you the skills and the mindset necessary to move on to the next task. It will be important for you to remember that you can know anything, but you can't know everything, and for you to gain mastery in your subject, it will require you to become a creator within your industry.

As you begin to learn more about yourself and your strengths, you'll start to find the things that you're most talented at, based on the things that your mind is consumed with. And once you find one or two things that you can spend all night doing, then that is where you start when you seek your purpose. There will never be an end to the pursuit of knowledge, because you can always learn something from someone else or from another experience. But you must be aware that as you go out into the world to seek knowledge, you must have discernment and know what is true and what is false, based on who wants to spread the truth and who wants to spread lies. The false prophets in your life will sometimes deliver a lie in a perfect package, trying to tempt you to believe in something that is against your value system, and it will be up to you to stand tall in your faith, and to know what is right beyond anything else.

False Prophets

There have been countless stories of men and women who have spread lies in order to gain power and riches at the expense of their people. If you think at a lower level of the people you see every day, who are trying to survive and make a living, you can see the same kind of behavior take place, where the knowledge of one person can be used to gain advantage of unknowing victims. Deception may be everywhere, so it'll be up to us to seek truth when everything we hear is a lie. The truth can be harder to uncover than a lie, and it's important to know the sacrifice it takes for the truth to be heard. The world operates on deception in order to keep the population subdued, but it allows a few at the top to control the laws of the rest of the world.

At this point in your journey, you will start to see false prophets in the form of the uneducated, the misunderstood, and the ignorant. Some people may spread lies in order to survive and feed their families, but others use that sport to gain power and influence. Therefore, it is important to make an impact within your craft to be a bearer of truth and to make the unpopular decisions that sometimes comes with it. To become aware of the false prophet that may be in your life, it is important to trust but verify everything that you hear, and to realize that no one has it all together. We begin our lives under the influence of our parents and guardians as a means of survival, and we look to them for the guidance necessary to get to the next stage of life, but we have to understand that they are imperfect people too, and their information may have been misdirected from someone else.

So, we must remain curious as we go along in life, because there's always a reason to question everything we hear, and the truth will find itself to us if we remain vigilant.

Knowledge

The biggest lie that I was told was that I will never change, and that I will always be screwed up, and will always be a troublemaker. It was not until 7th grade, in middle school, that I decided to make a change in my life. I told myself that there was more to who I was than being around the same kids that were going nowhere fast. I started to explore my talents in music and in poetry to keep me out of trouble. In high school, I played baseball and participated in track to stay away from the streets that took my dad at an early age. And I had to discover that the more I learned about my environment, the more I knew that the people around me were not leaders but were followers. When I decided to be a leader, I started seeing the same people that would fall victim to drugs and alcohol and become the false prophets that take so many youth in our communities.

You must trust your feelings when you are told instructions on how to live your life. Look at a person's body language; look at who they are, and what their character is. This will give you a hint whether they are there for your well-being or for their selfish desires. You will start to notice people and situations that you've seen before, and then you'll be able to discern between who is with you and who is against you. The mark of true intelligence in a person is whether they can learn new information and not let it shake their tree. You must be able to appreciate the person's knowledge based on their experiences and their life story. What is important to remember is that you don't have to change your beliefs for them. You can maintain your own values and belief system. You can appreciate that a word of wisdom was able to help them get to where they are in life but may not be the best advice for you. Once you can learn what your true value system is and understand that everyone in the world has a different experience of life, then you can find out what works for you and what doesn't. When you find your winning formula for the people and lessons that you need in order to learn and to get to the next level, then you will be able to really maximize your opportunities and find the right people to learn from.

True Intelligence

In today's information age, we have access to an unlimited amount of knowledge and data to equip us with all the tools necessary to be an expert in any field; but as a result, the flood of facts and opinions has disconnected us from the reality of wisdom and knowledge. Our generation has developed a sense of entitlement and instant gratification due to the increasing power of the internet, including social media. But the thing most people misunderstand is that our most important lessons transcend technology. The lessons of a lived experience give us more information in a moment than what can be explained in words. This is what we are missing out on: a world view that understands the fact that opinions cannot be believed without verifying its source. In order to progress in your journey to get to the next level in your craft, it will take the ability to discern between knowledge you need and information that draws away your focus.

I like to mention here about the dilemma with our current educational system. It is widely known that there is a gap between critical thinking and memorization of facts in the classroom. This has led to students lacking the basic

Knowledge

skills of self-rationalized thought to become creators instead of duplicators in their field of interest. A new perspective that needs to be introduced is to encourage our youth to work hand in hand with professionals, in the form of apprenticeship programs, in order to learn real-world skills and make immediate contributions as intelligent employees and entrepreneurs in today's workforce. Until educational reform can be accomplished to empower students to seek information at a younger age, there will be an increasing disparity between traditional learning and modern demands in the corporate environment. For all of us to take the matter in our own hands, it is important to become aware of your personal formula for success, in your unique pursuit of knowledge.

Think of the variety of information you learn at a grocery store: You shop for the things you need, based on your situation and experiences; and the information that does not serve you, you leave it where it is. This simple perspective can take the pressure off yourself to know everything all at once, which can seem overwhelming and unrealistic. Instead, strive to investigate information on your own. This will give you motivation to seek information as a habit and not a single event. There is something special about being a freethinker today, where you can truly look at new information from a subjective point of view and be able to look at things not as they are but for what they can be.

As you develop a vision for you and your family, you will be able to simplify your life and your choices with what aligns with what you believe in, and find sources of information that will show you the next step to accomplish your goals. This level of self-mastery will come once you are open to believing in your ability to trust but verify the lessons from your mentors for the self-preservation of your dreams. It will not be an overnight process to gain this view of the world, but it can be accomplished with the desire to be the best at what you do, and to understand that there is never one way to reach your goals. Your own intuition and feelings will lead you to gain a sense of what is right for you, and what is simply not a good fit for you at the time. Once you have the confidence to bet on yourself and your ability to search your feelings for the right answers, you will be able to emotionally detach yourself from the result and the need to know everything all at once, and become content with learning information that is necessary.

Emotional Intelligence

The widespread belief, which most people don't acknowledge, is that our mental health is a lifelong development process and needs attention regardless of a diagnosis from professionals. The true balance of life cannot be achieved without digging into all life experiences, and addressing your unique set of difficulties. You need to know how to properly function with your stress, for you to perform at a high-level. As *"the key to both personal and professional success,"* emotional intelligence is defined by Google as *"the capacity to be aware of, control, and express one's emotions, and to handle interpersonal relationships judiciously and empathetically."* In more simple terms, this is the ability to control your emotions around others during stressful situations. This section is by

Knowledge

far one of the most critical areas for you to master in order to reach your cruising altitude, since your unique definition of success cannot be accomplished alone. You will need a team of people to assist you on your journey, and it begins with admitting your weaknesses. Being able to keep your cool and see things from the other person's point of view will help you see the bigger picture on what kind of response is necessary for any given situation. If you can become aware of what triggers your responses, whether it is a certain person or a certain task that frustrates you, then you can manage those emotions before they have a chance to manifest negatively.

One of the first things new employers look for in their new hires is how they respond to new responsibility and pressure, so this is your opportunity for growth, and to handle stress you may not have experienced before. As you learn more about yourself and the things that make you happy, sad, mad, or excited, then you can try to control the choices you make to keep you in a balanced state. You want to strive to have the right emotions at the right time—during work, school, with friends or family—so you can attract others to your personality, and not repel them away. It will be natural not to respond appropriately every time in every situation, but becoming aware of how you respond will develop the habit of empathy within yourself, and give you the ability to see things from another's perspective in real-time. Experience will be your guide for this emotional pursuit of knowledge and your level of self-control through your failures. This lesson is rarely talked about in our schools and workplaces, but it is valuable for you to increase your influence among your peers.

A great suggestion I have learned from my mental health therapist is to always ask why. The intent is to seek the deeper meaning of how you think, and the way you respond. So, ask yourself, "Why did I respond that way?" Or, "Why did I act negatively toward that person or situation?" The mere fact that you have started to analyze how outside influences affect you, will show a great deal of maturity and personal growth on your part. I can be honest and tell you that there will be a lot of difficult conversations to get to a place of high EQ, but the beautiful thing about your journey is that you will become more confident in your choices to admit when you were wrong, and be more humble in moments when you are right. Your true victory will come when you manage to treat every first impression as a unique experience, because the circumstance doesn't take you back to past pain or agony in your lifetime. All of this cannot be done unless you take well-intended action to go and seek help about the past, and learn about how you respond when your mind takes you back to those places. When you take those few uncomfortable steps, and admit that you need help to find yourself again, then you can sit in a true power position by conquering the enemy within, and prepare yourself for the enemies outside of your environment. *Survival of the fittest* doesn't only depend on physical and mental strength; it depends on how people can adjust to constant change and adapt a new environment quickly.

Action

What is the one thing that attracts greatness in your direction—the thing that gets everything started when you put your plans down on paper? When we think about the most successful people in this world, there are common threads that tie them all together in one system of achievement, and that is clear and direct action toward their dreams and goals. This ingredient does not have to be overstated on why it is important, but few people are aware of how to use their actions to multiply the results of their efforts. Once you begin to seek your personal vision and purpose, you will find the craft or occupation that will lead you toward your destination. Once your path is clear, and you are aware of what needs to be done, this is where consistent effort takes place to cut your learning curve on your new journey. But where does action take part in all of this?

Think about the activities and exercises that you can do with the least amount of effort, that everyone around you knows that is your natural talent. When you attempt an effort in your natural talents and strengths, with confidence that you can accomplish your goal, then you are using willpower to amplify your efforts. *Effort* may be a conventional definition of your body and mind moving together to perform a deed, but within the navigator of knowledge, action is powered behind your self-belief and natural ability to take you to a place where time stands still or speeds up rapidly in order to surprise others around you. It is the habit of tapping into your identity and the miracles that are manifested because of your deeds within your spiritual self. There is a level of energy that is beyond human understanding, which can allow you to set yourself apart from your peers and give you the advantage in your chosen path of life.

When you take your actions into the spiritual, and plug into your eternal source, then you will be able to understand that your actions connect your mind, body, and spirit into a fluid system to make things around you come alive. This is where your opportunities that may seem outside your own logic come along, because you have performed an effort that is in the spiritual realm, and out of the normal physical world. This all will come with your understanding that there are supernatural occurrences in this world, from the greater Universe that is beyond human rational thought. Once you allow this information to become a part of you, then you can rest assured that your spiritual actions will align your innermost desires together with your practical goals. The Universe has a special way of moving us toward this level of effort, but we must first believe, then accept the path that it is taking us to, in order to take our talents to the next level. When I think about the unexplainable moments that came in my public speaking, I cannot conclude that it was scientific or practical, I can only reason that my actions started to communicate feelings and emotions that cannot be explained by words. This is the place where I seek to remain every time I speak in front of an audience, because it is where my true self can be shown, and where the English language cannot take me. As you begin to take the steps necessary to see the world outside of your city or country, then you can understand that over 7 billion spirits occupy this space, and there is a way we all communicate beyond verbal language. You can become skilled at anything you desire, with hard work and consistent effort, but when you figure out the 1 or 2 things that you can perform without breaking a sweat, then your personal miracles and dreams can come to life. You don't need to make your spiritual talents your job or professional career, but you would be naive to think that your life can be fulfilled without using your lifetime to benefit others by using these special gifts the Universe has given you.

Know Thyself

Dear reader, this journey of self-awareness and knowledge has led you to a point where, through this book, you have the necessary tools and insight to ask yourself the right questions to seek your purpose, strengths, weaknesses, mindset, and confidence to face your fears mentally and emotionally; but how do all these things work together to show you who you truly are? The answer lies in the moment you are born. Scientific studies have proven that we have a 1 in 400 trillion chance of being born in this moment in time. So, the odds of your life being meaningless and uneventful have even greater odds of being true. So, these two facts should empower you to realize that you have been placed on this earth to accomplish something that no one has seen before and will never experience again. As you tear down all the emotional baggage that has slowed you down up to this point, you can begin to be transparent with everyone you come across, and become an inspiration for everyone to see. The greatest example of love that you can show the world is within yourself, and the ability to not be of this world but to live in this world as an uncommon spiritual being.

There will be plenty of times where we extend ourselves to other people, and they let us down and disappoint us, but those learning moments are put in place for us to see life from a new perspective of strength and resilience. You must trust in the fact that as the Universe gives you the postulates of your dreams within your thoughts, that you have everything you need inside you to accomplish it and more, with the right amount of polishing and pressure to draw out the version of yourself necessary to handle the stress and responsibility it will take to handle these new challenges. Knowing thyself is the process you will embark upon when you decide to become something greater than what you see around you—the challenges that will break you down, and the lessons that will build you up again to face the same obstacles with the least amount of effort. It will take a lifetime and beyond to figure out the full nature of your spiritual being, but the good news is that once you begin to learn more about the true nature of your existence, you will see that life is simple and well-timed for your unique blessings and opportunities that will come into your life.

The day I made my decision to seek the answers within myself was in 2014, when I faced failure and rejection in business, and was let down by a client for an upcoming meeting. Overwhelmed with a feeling of confusion and sadness for another day without results, I took it upon myself to start asking what needs to be changed about my purpose and personality in order to deliver the result I wanted. I had no idea at the time that the failure and rejection was a part of my training to build up my resolve, and to teach me the lesson that business is 90% failure and 10% success, and that a warrior mindset will be needed to move forward, in spite of the rejections, and to

Knowledge

stay humble in the light of success.

As your life begins to unfold after the moment you make your decision, you will become more open-minded when you are facing high levels of stress and disappointment. You will now see that these experiences will soon become tools for you to tap into the purest form of your spiritual self and see that it will all lead you to learn about the real meaning of life and your definition of happiness. A feeling of service and gratitude will fill your heart as you become confident in the idea that you are on the right path, and nothing you face will distract you from it, because the people and circumstances you meet will have you on a natural high. The next chapter will explain how the respect of the Universe will assist you in seeing what is possible to be accomplished in your lifetime. Your personal power to reach your goal will depend on the omnipotent force of the Universe, and how it controls everything in and around us with perfect precision.

Chapter 6

Fear of Your Creator

*"Of all things visible,
the highest is the heaven of the fixed stars."*
– Nicolaus Copernicus

Faith

As our spirits continue to operate in the unseen, we are constantly witnessing events that can be described as unexplainable by conventional thought. Happenings in this world that come to reality due to man's singleness of thought can be concluded as having faith in this unseen realm. To explain things in a simple manner, faith can be described as the confidence in our unseen visions becoming concrete in the physical world. The sixth navigator begins with the lesson of faith, because your life is meant to reach heights that no man or circumstance can prevent. This can also relate to our sixth sense with the ability to see the end as we begin a new adventure.

The sequence of my events leading to the writing of this book is tied to my personal belief that I was meant to promote and endorse an idea that would reach a world audience. I had no way of seeing the process between the point of this idea beginning and the wisdom I possess, but I had confidence that powers outside of my control would lead me to my initial idea, and let life take care of the rest. In the Christian religion, there is a story of the Israelites undergoing a forty-year journey, from the shackles of slavery, to reach a promised land that stood against all rational thought among the people. Only God himself knew the end purpose of their journey, and He used the prophet, Moses, as an imperfect leader, to show the omnipotent power of God, to move nations in his favor. Today, the masses of the world have depended on scientific data and reasoning for the miracles that happen every day, in order to properly explain the unseen. This is where your life can take on new meaning as you begin to follow the signs that work in your favor in order to be more in tune on what the Universe is telling you, and to take the reins on your existence. As you counsel with older generations before you, there will be knowledge and wisdom that you must learn about the true power of the Universe, which will give you hints on how to choose between good and bad decisions, bringing you closer to the life you desire. By using the smallest bit of faith in your decisions, you will begin to see that the decisions you make will seem crazy to others that do not see what you see, as your vision was a gift for you, and you alone.

There is something to be said about *a job* and *work*— two ideas that most people confuse on the purpose and direction of their lives. A job is a way to make a living to support yourself and your family, but a life's work is an undertaking that the Universe has selected for you to accomplish during the short time you are on this earth. It will be up to you to choose to follow this path to fruition, and to have confidence that wherever it takes you will be for the benefit of yourself and the Universe. There is a perfect timeline of events that will unfold as you use your power of faith that will open doors that only have your name on it. And the sooner that you relax and come to peace with being led instead of controlling every detail of your life, the faster these opportunities will come your way, to build and mold you into the best version of yourself.

This section is not a guarantee that your hard work will lead you to the destination that you plan, but a declaration that the work you do will be rewarded in perfect timing to give you what you need and not what you want. There are no words that can explain the unseen events that will happen in your life, and it may take a lifetime to learn the reasons why you suffered the pain and challenges in your life; but the first step in trust will take you to becoming vulnerable to what is in store for you and the people that you will one day influence. Faith without works will die in the same place it started, unless you move your mindset to the unseen, and act.

Planning and Being Led

"Piss poor preparation promotes piss poor performance!" There is no doubt about it that your life cannot be executed to your liking without a plan in place to execute with strict discipline and endurance. There is always a motivator that moves people to do the boring and mundane tasks on the road to their heart's desire, but it may vary for you and your experiences. I try to think of adulthood as a boring routine that leads to exciting moments in life. This is where we choose to take responsibility and accept the path to get to a level of greatness. It doesn't make you outdated or boring as a person, but discipline in the daily tasks of your craft is sharpening your skills, keeping you hungry over your competitors, and staying sharp for any new challenges that arise. It is imperative that you set daily, weekly, and monthly goals for the progress of your vision, and this will keep you on track to be able to see the end every day. But what happens when you miss your goals, or life brings you a new opportunity that would show you a new way of doing things? What happens when you hit a roadblock that derails you from the initial dream you seek, and forces you to course correct your whole journey?

This is the difference between *planning your life* and *being led in your life*, where you set your plans in motion, but you allow the Universe to present you with the next step, staying flexible to the changing conditions of life, and thinking about the end in mind the whole time. This way of thinking can lead a lot of people on the road to depression because it takes away everything they want and delivers what they need, having no idea that the latter may be the best alternative compared to the former. There is a lot of instant gratification within our generation due to the emergence of technology and social media, and we are having trouble coping with the fact that we cannot attain the life of our dreams in a moment's notice. There must be a shift in our perspective that life is dependent on choices, but those choices may not be presented until we are ready to receive them. For entrepreneurs, for example, the choice to start a business and leave your full-time job goes against all conventional wisdom within corporate America. But the desire to create something new was a process that started from smaller decisions that came from chance or intuition. At the end of the day, the big decisions we make, come from the series of small decisions that exposed us to what life could be, and to explain how these series of events tied together in perfect harmony is outside of our conventional thinking.

There are moments in time when we must follow the signs in front of us and think about what will happen if we refuse to follow what we are being told to do with our life choices. Because it does not matter who you are, life will find its way of using you for its divine purpose, but we do have a choice whether to be a vessel or a weight to slow ourselves down in the natural flow of the world. A step you can take to start becoming aware of the power of being led is in your meditation. Ask yourself the question: "Who is deciding my path for me?" This will open your subconscious mind to the possibility of who is truly controlling your life decisions, and if you are seeking validation from others or choosing your path on your own. This is very important to understand, to ensure that you are the captain of your own ship, and that no one else is driving for you.

The next question you should ask yourself is, "Why am I choosing to live this life?" This thought-provoking question will help your mind find the true reason that you are on your path; pay attention to the feeling that comes to mind when you see the signs showing your answer. This can give you more insight on a course correction that you may not want, but it is necessary to ensure fulfillment for the long-term plan to be successful.

The Great Struggle

As you allow yourself to be led by your feelings, and not by the material items of the world, there will be challenges that you must face in order to see the blessings that are on the other side of fear. This is a great challenge all of us must face in order to test our faith and spiritual being to its absolute limit. I call this period of time "the great struggle," an ordeal that will strengthen your resolve to see the true power of the Universe working in direct connection with a world that is built to distract you from your focus on the pursuit of your true purpose. Most people live in lack due to their unwillingness to learn from the lessons of their struggles, and to have them serve as a living testimony, and to equip themselves to use their pain as a catalyst for a change inside, to allow the world to see their true light. There is no way of telling when and where this lesson will begin or end, but one thing can be certain, and that is that you will have to break through these barriers in order to have your breakthrough and become the person who you are meant to be. Think about the number of people in the world that pray to be in your position, and the extent they would go through to live your life today. Everyone starts at different places in this world and must go through great lengths in order to thrive within their surroundings. Your willingness to be open-minded and see each day as an opportunity for growth will show the value of your darkest days, to become a beacon of light for others to follow.

During my time in college, in 2012, I was faced with a tough decision: to have food to eat or gas money to drive to school. It forced me to become resourceful in my greatest moment of discomfort and fear, but it was necessary for me to learn how to survive under any circumstance. Because of this life-changing experience, it gave me the confidence to go out on my own and be comfortable with taking calculated risks, to find ways to create new ways to make money as I built my empire.

There are forces that must test your personal resilience before giving you the responsibility of a new lifestyle, to ensure you are able to handle great power and influence when you have everything, by seeing how you react when you have nothing. When we think about the great struggle in the form of peaks and valleys, we must think about who we are at the beginning of the journey. This is the point where, as we start to slip and fall, we leave the person that we were, and we start to think of the things we lacked as we go down to the valley. Then we start to think about what we are as we hit our lowest point in the deepest darkest places of our mind, and we must decide whether to fight or to allow life to keep us paralyzed. This is when we start to figure out the person that is truly within us, and it is drawn out to be able to meet the challenge ahead of us, one step at a time. Finally, as we rise out of our struggle and start to feel the first inkling of success, we figure out *why* we are, and this is the lesson that we learned after the test, where we understand the purpose for undergoing a distressful ordeal. The lesson that is meant to be learned is not just for us but is for people that will follow the same path, and it may be up to us to encourage them to draw out the best versions of themselves when they believe they can't fight anymore.

Everyone's struggles come in different forms—from identity crisis, mental trauma, lack, or addiction, to material possessions—but the process will always be the same. To figure out who, where, and why, gives us clarity and prepares us for the next challenge. They may seem a bit easier, but it is in fact us who have become stronger and more able to handle the pressure and the responsibility of a new way of life.

Your Purpose

There is no greater feeling in the world than finding out the reason for your existence. It gives us a full circle view of our place in the world, and provides us new opportunities that we would never see before. Fulfillment is a feeling of being complete as a human being, and the focus it gives you to seek your maximum potential once you see the path to take to achieve it. In the same vein, it is also an enormous responsibility to carry as well. When we think of the people who have pushed our society forward, it was never a clear path to the greatness they would go on to achieve. The personal struggles and stories not recorded in our history books or shown by the news media were the battles of quiet chaos that we all face at times. The moments of self-doubt, to the feeling of quitting when morale is low, is part of the process of staying the course to find your true place in the Universe. It is from my very own experience that I would submit to you that you have a purpose to live out, whether you know it or not. The idea that is important to note is how your significance works in the bigger plan of the world around us. If everyone is led to believe that we all will live out a materially wealthy lifestyle once we figure out our purpose, we will be placed on a path of destruction, because we set ourselves up for failure when life does not give us the reality we desired. We should strive for joy and balance when we seek our unique identities and become fascinated with the day that we can become freethinkers, with the ability to assist others in whatever capacity we desire.

In my mid-twenties, I started to reflect on the reason why I loved to challenge myself and endure uncomfortable conditions to force myself to grow. There was no logical explanation on why I always sought to embarrass myself by learning something new, or why I focused on myself as my greatest competition. But when I started to learn how adaptable I became in my talent of speaking and communication, it started to click for me on why I dealt with the struggle to find myself. It was in order to validate my need for becoming the authority in any field I involved myself in, forcing me to learn quickly and use my past failures as fuel to push past my fear of loss, and risk more for a bigger reward. In doing that, I began to see that the few others, like myself, deal with the constant pressure they place upon themselves to find their purpose as well.

But if we take a step back and remain in the present, we can see that your purpose does not have to be figured out at this moment. The Universe has a mysterious way of preparing us before placing this great test in our lives, by allowing us to learn how to be still in the present moments we have and develop ourselves for that one special assignment to push humans forward. Instead of asking yourself the question, "What am I here on this earth to do?" begin with a question your mind can answer in the present moment, such as, "What can I do to make today successful?" This idea brings you to a deeper level of your natural talents and abilities, and places you on a track where you remove *analysis paralysis*—the overwhelming feeling when your mind has too much information to process all at once.

By remaining focused on day to day activities, and taking time to reflect on the long-term goals, you reach a level of freedom where decisions become simpler, the people you surround yourself with change their minds or change places, and you start becoming content with the position you are in. This is where your purpose begins to manifest itself, because you become at peace with your place in the world. Before you can figure out the assignment you have been brought to this world for, it will be important to become emotionally and mentally balanced, and to start to see life as a vessel, so that the power of the Universe can flow through you as miracles start to happen around you.

A Vessel

In a recorded studio interview with Bruce Lee, during his acting career in America, he explains the importance of being formless, like water: As the water is placed in a cup, it becomes the cup, taking its shape and form. When we think of how to flow as water, we need to understand the idea of being fluid in our actions with the events of our life. This is not an easy concept by any means, but it can be done if we think about what comes naturally, and then place ourselves in alignment with the service of the greater good and what that means to us. Once you establish a habit of meditation and reflection on your daily formula for success, you will need to search your feelings and being to see everything as a lesson, and not as a burden to carry with you.

The power of water, as one of the elements of this earth, is its power to replenish and give life, but by the same token, it can take life away, and serve as a destructive force of nature. In the end, water is flowing in its natural capacity, and performs as a vessel for the plan of the Universe, to carry it out in perfect timing and order. There is never a right or wrong answer on why we are chosen for the assignments we are given to live out, but it is in perfect harmony with our existence to become a vessel of the Universe, and to allow ourselves to live the life that is in natural flow of our world, and avoid forcing ourselves into a lifestyle or status that robs us of our dignity and morals. One of the greatest disappointments that we see frequently is in people that show so much promise and potential to become a positive influence in their communities, only to have it taken away by their own negligence or acts of violence that rob them of their lives before the world could see their unique work of art.

We never know when our time on this side of life is going to end, or when our circumstances are changed forever by a lone phone call, but it will be up to us to encourage others to seek this life of service in their own expressive form, and to remind others who they truly are. When you think of how to become a vessel for the service to others around you, start with the things you can give today, such as time or money. If time is all you have, your service may lie in your interests and becoming a leader to others in expressing themselves in the same way; if your contributions will come in money or resources, who could you help to equip them for success?

It doesn't take you to begin a movement to begin living within the power of the Universe; it only takes your willingness to become a gateway for others to see opportunities they would not have seen without you. Helping the world around you may become a thankless job after a while, but it will be important that you thank yourself with your own form of self-care in order to recharge and contribute to the interests that flow with your values and beliefs, because a vessel cannot help anyone if it is empty! It becomes important that you remain humble during this process and understand that the unexplainable happenings that occur outside of your understanding is the power of the Universe and not necessarily your own effort and actions. When we begin to take credit for the supernatural, we allow pride and ego to drive our decisions instead of love and gratitude. This can become a destructive path that will re-align us to balance, but the damage would already be done to our relationships, lifestyle, and emotional health. So, when people thank you for your efforts, and praise you for the unique things you bring to this world, it's important to remain grounded in being the vessel of the Universe and seek the next action every step of the way.

Back to the Source

When religious leaders speak on the idea of personal growth, they relate the highest form of existence as the embodiment of its originator or prophet that all their disciples study under. This is because when you direct a group's way of thinking to a person instead of an idea, it becomes relatable and easier to attain. But too many times, people in the world's religions start to idolize the messengers instead of the message. When you place your faith in a person instead of a mindset, you begin to doubt your values if you see the imperfect character of your religious leader. Therefore, it is important to always attach yourself with evolving your ideas and perspective on life, instead of reaching the destination of men and women that you may idolize. You have to understand that you are in fact the person you idolize, because you attach your personal values to them, and when you begin to see other people that are perfectly imperfect, you start to believe in yourself, to evolve past that point, to reach a level of *imperfect perfection*.

This concept stems from the idea of going on a journey to truly know yourself above anyone else. As you continue to commit yourself to your own self-evolution, while maintaining your connection to the Universe, you reach a level of self-mastery, where money doesn't matter anymore, status is inconsequential, and moments of pride are seen from a mile away. And the special thing about imperfect perfection is that it comes in a moment when you relinquish the need to control everything in your life. This is the time in your life when you begin to give control to the Universe, when things are unclear, because that is when you consume your mind and things that you cannot control, and bring yourself unnecessary stress that inhibits rational thought. In simpler terms, if there is nothing you can do to change the past or your present situation, then allow life to work out the details, and save yourself the headache.

Plugging back into our source is more than meditation and prayer; it is a mindset that allows us to be free from the attachment of results, and to become interested in the process of how we approach the details of our lives. It is a special thing where we start to accept the idea that there is always a better way to accomplish a goal, because we place ourselves in a position of progress, where we are open to change. As the world changes around us, we must be willing to reinvent ourselves as necessary, and avoid drifting through life if we are forced to change our approach to move forward.

For you to reconnect back to the source of your spiritual being, start to ask yourself, "What things can I affect in this present moment?" Write them down if necessary. Everything else that you can't change with your actions or attitude, then you must relinquish control of those events. You will begin to see that the things we have a direct impact to influence are few, and you will remember that the greatest thing we can impact is how we see others around us. When you stop expecting everyone to act like you, then you will be able to see everyone's unique way of thinking as a gift to them, and not as a burden on yourself.

Fear of Your Creator

    The most important idea you can learn from this chapter is that the Universe is always conspiring to assist you along the way, and that everything happens *for* you, and not only *to* you. When you keep this idea in your mind, then you can start to see that the things outside of your control are in fact guiding your personal decisions on who to meet, where to go, and what to do. It will be critical that you understand that the Universe will not always give you favorable conditions to live in, but it will reward you for pushing through those times of difficulty and remaining faithful to your natural flow of joy and fulfillment. Once you are able to find happiness in any situation, then you can rest assured that you will attract others around you, and you will become their source of inspiration, and it is in this moment that you will need to direct them to the true source of gratitude by educating them on the fear of your creator.

    In the next chapter, we discuss the final navigator to take your life to cruising altitude. The spirit of your creator is the many forms of love and acceptance of others. But it comes at a cost to love at the level of universal creation, and if you're willing to accept this lifestyle, then you will be shown a world that only a few people have the vision to experience.

Chapter 7

The Spirit of Your Creator

"Be faithful to that which exists within yourself."
– Andre Gide

Unconditional Love

What idea do you think of when you think about unconditional love for another person? And does this idea involve your feelings toward who someone is, or your feelings about what they do? The spirit of your creator may come as a different idea, depending on who you are, but the message that I would like to communicate to you is that your creator is relatable to you in every part of your life. There is no force on this earth that understands you more than the being that brought you here in the first place. For some people, the creator is in the form of a prophet, a deity, or nothing at all; but a higher level of thinking can lead us to understand the power of creation. To bring you to this moment, the history of the world was formed out of love.

Regardless of the circumstances of how you were conceived, creation in its purest form thrives as an imposing force to fear and lack. Just as our enemies feed off our own insecurities, we have the power to feed the goodness in our hearts by falling in love with the power of our existence, in any condition. The unconditional love that you may seek from other people will have to start with loving yourself in your reality, before anything else. When you think about the purest form of an idea, it comes as a known unknown, meaning that you can sense the potential in how things can be better, but you may not be sure of the exact way to get there. The appreciation for the way you evolve every time life brings you an obstacle, is the way that your creator can love who you are in any condition during this process. There will be times when loving who you are and loving others will seem impossible to do, because you may face fear and guilt from broken relationships or unmet expectations. But it is the will to find the silver lining, and to love what has happened to you, and to learn to turn love into an action verb, and give yourself repeatedly to your goal of self-mastery, whether it's through people or through your spiritual source.

The true lesson of the 7 navigators cannot be applied unless you choose to express love in your own special way and avoid allowing fear to stop your personal growth. Since you live under the principles of righteousness, you begin to see that love and fear cannot exist without each other, and it will be your choice on how you approach life, but it is not guaranteed that you will face the opposing force that you fight against. There will be times that fear will creep into your heart, leaving you restless and unsure about yourself, but this will be natural for you to feel the purpose of loving who you are outside of your comfort zone.

It becomes hard to love people when they don't think about your feelings as they mistreat you, because you don't expect them to respond negatively to your act of love towards them. When you tie your happiness to the actions of others around you, you choose the uncertainty of fear over the divine love for yourself first, so you can remove your emotions and expectations about another person's actions. You have to remember that your creator loved you so much that they shifted the world to make room for you, and when you refuse to take responsibility for your own love and happiness, you begin to seek an internal emotion from an external source, which can change the lens of how you see things around you. This is where you will need to find the small group of people that will always direct you back to the idea to love yourself before anything else in your day-to-day choices. These angels within your life will begin to open your mind on what is possible, and keep you grounded when pride and ego begin to affect your relationships in personal life. It will be important to seek out the people that love themselves enough to love you in return, and learn how to overflow your love onto others, and not depend on them to fill you up.

Your Angels

Who is single-handedly responsible for saving your life? Who was the person that turned your life around when you least expected it? These 2 questions may not be answered by the time you finish reading this section, but I would like you to think about the people that only see the best in you and never look for a reason to leave you. The Universe works through people, and there is an unusual amount of love that they share with you that we sometimes neglect. As you take time to think about those angels in your life, imagine where we would be if everyone thought of themselves and never thought of other people. The media always gives us the impression that evil is consuming this world, but the fact is, when you think about life outside of basic survival, you will begin to see others around you that commit themselves to love and not fear.

As life applies pressure to you, and you set out to make your dreams come true, there will be a period of time where you will find out who your true friends are, the people that see past your status, money, and popularity. What do you do then, when the people you thought were your friends leave you high and dry, and you are left with only your parent, relative, or mentor to talk to? You begin to find your angels during your times of difficulty, before or during the great struggle; but it will be up to you to have an open mind, not toward the people that you've known the longest, but toward the people who value your opinions and feelings. You can consider this special group of people as your lifeline that supports you beyond money or shelter. These will be the individuals that will lift your spirits when you're down. They will remind you of who you are when you forget the person you're becoming. It will be crucial to be transparent and clear in your intentions on what you are going through personally, because if we lie to ourselves, then we only slow down our own progress.

Don't be fooled into thinking that the person that may provide you council will always be your selected angel, because when your means are limited, then you will have to lean on people who don't expect anything in return, and this is a lifetime bond that money can't buy. When I think of my personal angels, I begin with my mother, since she was a person who always stayed by my side during my most confusing times of my childhood, where it could have been easy to give up on me. There is something special about a mother's love that shows children the everlasting power of unconditional love. And now, when I face new challenges, I can always rest assured that she will give me her best insight based on my best interest, and I can remain confident in decisions that I make.

Even if there's nobody that comes to mind when you think of your anointed angel, it will be important to continue your journey and allow the right people to be attracted to you as you show your initiative in giving love to others. If you set your mind to creation, then you will be able to understand that forces on this earth have been sent to protect your vision, and you always have a way out when you feel all alone.

A Creator

However, you feel that this world was created, you must admit that there was a predetermined event that existed beforehand. Whether you believe it was God himself or the big bang theory, there was careful placement of how everything was set into motion, which makes us wonder how everything in the Universe can operate in perfect harmony. How can we explain that special moment when an idea forms in our minds from nothingness, and we see how ideas and physical objects can be manipulated to form a new item for a new purpose. We have gravely underestimated ourselves and how we think, and what we are capable of doing during our time here. Your power of creation doesn't end with your thoughts and physical objects; it begins with that moment of inspiration—those epiphanies that trigger everything in motion, and when you are able to channel the creative power into something positive, there is no force in the world that can take it away.

We have seen, countless times, the destructive power of pride and ego, and how it can destroy nations and civilizations. But throughout the history of time, there have been the thinkers and the visionaries who have risen despite the oppressors that try to silence them. And their creative power to generate something out of thin air is the true purpose of progress, to allow our power of creation, to remind others around us of who we really are. As a creative being in this world, you have the ability to become anything that you set your heart to; but the true test that you will face as you seek your heart's desire is whether you will allow your creative force to guide you on your path, or whether you will stay in your comfort zone and allow life to pass you by.

This can be one of the tough decisions that we have to make: whether to trust those instincts that seem outside of our natural way of thinking, or to follow them and allow courage to push us through those uncomfortable situations within our minds and emotions. You have to understand that you share the same creative nature of the Universe, because you were made out of the Universe, and you have been cut from a fabric of the infinite, to a point that there is no beginning and end to your ability, but you have to acknowledge your faith in the world to deliver the solutions that you seek. When you rest at peace in your life, and you begin to see the beauty in the present moment, then you are taking your mind to another plane of thinking. You are allowing your mind to be open to expansion, because once you push your mind past a point of growth, you will never go back to the level of thinking you had before.

The moment when I became aware of my creative abilities was in middle school, when I started to play violin. There was something special that I saw between the notes every time I played, which gave me a love for music, and whenever I would perform at a concert with my orchestra mates, I could feel the emotions in each moment, where the music wasn't just sound but started becoming a state of being for me. I didn't understand how or why I gravitated toward music at a young age, but it showed me what was possible for my mind, and it gave me an escape from school. It took me to another place, where no one existed but me and my violin, to express myself in a way where words could not go. It showed me that there is a language that we all speak, in different forms that everyone can understand. And later in life, I used that same ability to channel my energy into things that drew me closer to my creator, and when I can't find the words to explain it, that's when my emotions paint the picture for me.

There are no guarantees when you will find your creative muse, but one thing that you can stand behind is the fact that this power rests within you, and it will be up to you to draw it out, and it will be in perfect timing with your existence. It will take a special kind of person to be willing to stand out in front and face criticism everywhere to find the one thing that makes their heart sing, and if you are willing to take on this challenge, then you have the qualities to lead others on the same path, to show them what is available for them.

A Leader

Success magazine quotes Jack Welch on a unique idea on leadership:

"Before you are a leader, success is all about growing yourself. When you become a leader, success is all about growing others."

Mister Welch makes a great point on being able to develop yourself before you can develop others. Imagine a Fortune 500 company that employs people just like you, with the same character, the same motivation, and the same passion. Where would your company be in 10 years? In a more spiritual sense, the Universe is always evolving and growing into the best version of itself possible, through correction, and we must understand that correction comes in different forms—a physical change within nature, or mental changes within people. There will always be a period of self-development in order to handle the responsibility of being a leader, and this is the point in time when you must embrace the discipline it takes in working toward excellence, day in and day out. Leadership can mean leading from the front or taking care of your people, but in order to grow into that person that has compassion for the people he or she is leading, you must become an example for them to follow. The spirit of the Universe always creates an environment where the cream of the crop rise and see changes that need to be made within the world, and as our true leaders come to power, we must look to them not only for what they did but for their mindset on their path to greatness.

It's not every day that we learn about leadership in school or in the workplace, but we can always point to examples to teach us how to build a solid foundation, whether we believe we are leaders are not. If you have been led to read this book today, you are in fact a leader. Now it is your responsibility to find out where and when to be the person you're supposed to be in order to push us all forward. You don't have to speak on a podium in front of thousands of people to be a leader, nor do you have to lead a company that makes millions of dollars a year. It starts with the desire to learn more around you, and to become more involved in the activities that you have an interest in, because now you're making decisions not only for yourself but for the people that look at you as an example in your craft and in your personal life.

My mother told me throughout my childhood that I was meant to be a leader, and that my friends would always follow me no matter where I went. I didn't understand what she saw back then, but when I started to realize it for myself, I did not accept the responsibility. I was afraid of letting myself and my family down if I were to make a mistake leading the pack. But after graduation from the University of Southern California, I saw that being a leader isn't by being placed in a box. A leader thinks beyond the industry they are part of, and people can follow them when they are being their genuine selves and dedicating their lives to the craft. Because legends don't follow two masters, they have a clear idea of who they need to be, and they maximize as much time as they can to build tools to develop new skills, meet new people, create new ideas, and allow their lives to be transformed by the renewing of their minds.

As the spirit of your creator navigates you toward the responsibility of leadership within your craft, you must learn to accept it, not as the end of an exciting life but as the beginning of freedom. When we're young, life begins to show us freedom in a limited form, but if you commit yourself to something that can truly free you from the life of quiet desperation, then you can be free to make decisions that are not limited by money or time. You can make decisions based on purpose and vision, which can affect thousands of people's lives without even being on a TV screen. You can shake the world gently, only if you first commit to growing yourself.

An Example

Regardless of the circumstance, success will always leave clues. But the unique difference between following a man or a woman or following the infinite intelligence of the Universe, is that the example comes when there is no blueprint to follow. The most beautiful thing about it is that you have a chance to be able to do something that hasn't been done before. The spirit of your creator establishes an example to follow, not based on what you see around you but according to inspiration, imagination, and perfect balance. You must understand that there are things that we can attach ourselves to that are beyond our five senses, and that your 6th sense is activated when you can feel an awareness of what the Universe is trying to show you. It can be in the form of a sign, showing you the next decision to make, or it can be in the form of resources that have been given to you for some unexplainable reason. So, the idea that you must understand about how the spirit of your creator provides examples, is by the power of duplication and simplicity.

When you try to complicate the order of balance in the world, then you disrupt a natural flow that everything works under. The best things in life are simple and duplicable, not because it's easier but since more people can grasp the concept faster. Some examples in this sense may include stories that everyone knows, or a simple task such as tying your shoes, but when you think of it on a larger scale, think of how the simple act of accomplishing your dream starts with the simple act of thinking about it. Although these actions come up, the desire to want more always starts with an example to follow in order to guide you on your path. This is where your angels and mentors will be able to assist you, so learn how to stay in tune with yourself, and then look for the signs that speak to you spiritually.

When I look back on the examples in my life, of how the Universe assisted me, I think of the opportunities that came out of my challenges, because there was always a story or a person to look at that had accomplished everything that

I've desired. When I imagined myself on a higher level of existence, I tried to attach the idea to something that I could relate with, and whether you believe it is human biology or natural instinct, we have this unique ability of attachment within the physical laws of the Universe. As humans, we always must attach pictures and words to ideas that are unfamiliar to us in order to understand the concepts.

A question you could begin to ask yourself is, "What do I desire more than anything else?" Then take some time to think about the closest idea that can be attached to your desire, because you may be surprised that what you desire most will not always be attached to another person; it can be a feeling, an object, or an experience. That first foundation of thought is what you need to see the true power of your creator. If the idea was placed into your mind, then the means of acquiring this desire is there for you to draw upon.

We always must make decisions out of love to align ourselves with our true potential of our existence, and one thing we can always count on is the source of inspiration that exists in the world. No matter the challenge or position that you are in life, there will always be someone or something to draw strength upon to move you past your levels of depression or fear. There's something unique about the human spirit, where it constantly shows true resilience regardless of the circumstance, and it will show us people who have traveled the same path so that we can learn how to pick ourselves back up and start over again if necessary. You must learn to always look for simplicity in duplication and what you see around you. I understand that the longer you live on this earth, the more patterns you will see to gain experience in wisdom on what to do for your next step.

A Guide

As I stated in the beginning of this book, the 7 navigators serve as a guide in order to direct you to a higher calling or the best version of yourself. But in the spirit of your creator, a guide becomes a North Star for you to follow in your morals and values. As the world continues to fill with drifters that have no direction, our path to follow will be up to people like you and me, in order to stand up and show people the idea of following something bigger than themselves. It can be said that faith is uncomfortable at times because it puts us in uncomfortable positions, and we sometimes feel lost or abandoned, but a guide is not there to tell you the destination. A guide's purpose is to lead you step by step through eminent danger, to show you the path the few will travel.

In the span of my lifetime, my life consisted of friends and family, but during uncertainty and when I was left to make a decision alone, it was that instinct in my conscience that told me the right answer, and after spending countless hours worrying about the solution to a problem, I allowed myself to let go and acknowledge that the whole idea of the Universe creating us was to allow ourselves to be guided back to the unconditional force of love. As we choose to follow the steps that make the most sense to us, we begin to figure out the easy path that may lead to complacency, or the difficult road that will lead some to greatness. There are some of us that love a good challenge, who will never back down when they are forced to act decisively. But when we are faced with no more options, and we're out of resources, we must follow the first instinct that showed us the way when we didn't want to listen.

It is important to mention the destructive nature of pride and ego, because it creates an illusion that we are leading ourselves, when the future is unpredictable for everyone. As I stated before, it's always important to have a strategy when being led, so when it's time to decide between sticking with your plan and following unconventional wisdom to be led, your guide is that voice that speaks beyond logic and allows you to open your mind to more possibilities available. It will serve as your comforter when you feel heartache, and it will give you peace when your mind is full of chaos. When you acknowledge that the Universe is everywhere at once, then you can understand that you were placed here to reach a higher level of consciousness, and the Universe will serve as your compass to align you with the people and circumstances needed to challenge you, and it will be your free will to accept the challenge and trust this guide to show you the answers only when necessary.

The greatest exercise of following your guide will be during transition periods. When there is a new relationship, a new job, or a new place to live, this is when you must become the most in tune with the Universe, and meditate on what you need to do in order to know the next step. Your guide will serve as your conscience, giving you intuition and insight into some of your most difficult challenges. You can rest assured that there is always someone who has existed that has done the same challenges that you are facing, and if they can do it so can you.

In our final chapter, we will cover the moment that you give yourself to the Universe, and you start to see what your life is truly capable of. As you begin to ascend to cruising altitude, you will start to see life from a higher perspective. Your decisions won't be based on lack, and you will have love and abundance to share with everyone around you; but in order to maintain your love with your existence, you must be aware of some of the pitfalls that will come, or it will come crashing down, and you will be forced to start over again.

Chapter 8

Cruising Altitude

"The power of imagination makes us infinite."
— John Muir

A New Universe

New beginnings always start with a feeling of peace, and when you have achieved this peace, it makes things a little clearer. You reflect on the past, and a feeling of gratitude is usually the overwhelming feeling, because you remember how far you came to get where you are, and all the failures seem like an investment instead of a loss.

What happens after you have finally achieved the thing that you lived your life for, and you don't know where to go from there? Complacency is a dangerous feeling, because you lose your edge and the hunger that got you there; but when you change your mindset from sprinting to marathons, you can realize that every experience is neither good nor bad. The two words become relative in regard to how you see each situation, and you start to see the novelty in each memory. The blessings you once prayed for begin to become easy, with minimum effort, and the challenges you feared the most become routine habits that you wouldn't bat an eye at anymore. So how do we keep sharp as we finally reach the achievement that we have worked so hard for all these years? The answer lies in a quote from the poem, "IF," by Rudyard Kipling:

"If you can dream –
and not make dreams your master;
If you can think – and not make thoughts your aim,
If you can meet with Triumph and Disaster
And treat those two impostors just the same . . ."

Dreams, thoughts, victory, and defeat are all experiences that everyone on this earth shares, but it is the most successful beings on this planet that stay calm through each emotion. It is apparent as you ascend to a new level that you keep your head about you, and you understand that there is always a higher level to go to, and there is always a destination to see. There is a quality of being confident in the fact that you belong wherever the Universe places you, and that you do have a say in whatever room you place yourself into. As you begin to gain experience in each new world that you enter, then you start to realize that your mind is like water—it's formless and shapeless, but it takes on the new shape of the new experience. Your mind molds around it, and for it to become solid, and to get the maximum amount of opportunities and resources that you will need for the next step, you must begin to immerse yourself repeatedly.

Cruising Altitude

There is a moment when a pilot/captain tells everyone that they are safe to unbuckle their seatbelts and move around the cabin, indicating that they have reached cruising altitude, a level where most think the ride will become smoother because there is no agitation, no shakiness, and no chaos; but reaching cruising altitude means that you now have the ability to see more things at once, and you will now have the opportunity to travel to whatever goal or destination that you desire. But in order to get there and to immerse yourself within each culture, there must be adjustments made, and there must be preparation for the unpredictable. This is always a time to celebrate, because you have reached a level that few people even get to see in their lifetimes. But It is very important to stay focused on your mission because, when you find your purpose, there will be plenty of pitfalls to slow you down or derail you. New challenges will always come your way; that's an undeniable fact of life, but what we need to do is to remain calm and start to focus on how to handle our new blessings with the same hunger and desire that got us to this point.

Turbulence

Success has a mysterious way of leaving you unguarded from future challenges, because it places you in a position of comfort that may soon lead to complacency in your business, job, or education. Even at the highest levels of achievement, you'll be faced with challenges that can threaten everything you work for, if you're not careful. There will never be a time when your life will be void of problems, and you must learn to manage these problems in order to maintain a balance and keep showing up at work, school, or in your relationships. When you change your perspective on how you see turbulence and cruising altitude, then you will realize that there is something positive about going through a high pressure situation. It will only come with persistent faith in the Universe, and knowledge that your creator has given you the tools necessary to overcome any obstacle that you will face in your life. You can be confident in the fact that the things that you pray for today may become the challenges you face tomorrow, because every blessing contains a curse.

Now we must learn to cope with both in order to learn the necessary lessons to reach the next level. My time in graduate school was filled with joyful memories but also stressful nights where I was uncertain that I would be successful, but thanks to my cohort, they were able to show me that you just need to show up every time. When I was overwhelmed with the feeling of uncertainty about what path to take in my life, there was always someone to remind me who I was and what I was made of; and I would begin to think of the nights when I had prayed to be in a position to earn a Master's degree, and to reach a new level of achievement where you can pick your path and not allow others to choose it for you.

It is said that less than 5% of people put in the effort to write down their goals, so it is no surprise then that less than 5% of people control 95% of the world's wealth. Make no mistake; even the world's most wealthy people go through problems at their level, and there must be a way that they can maintain a balance while showing up every day and performing at a high level. We must begin by asking ourselves the questions: "What did I pray for before I faced this problem?" And, "Is the thing that I want based on happiness or joy?" If you are able to remember the things that you once prayed for, you can show gratitude within your circumstance, and find a joy in figuring out the solutions to your problems.

Dear reader, as you continue along your path, you must realize that life will operate in peaks and valleys, and when you look back from your greatest struggle, and you deal with small turbulence at your highest level, there will be an overwhelming amount of peace and gratitude that will consume your mind, and you will wonder why you were so worried, because you were covered on all fronts. When the enemy tries to keep you from seeing what is in front of you, you can believe that you are already covered, and when people in your life try to blindside you and take everything away from you, you can believe that you are already covered. When you're facing outside challenges, and you don't have the skills or the knowledge to complete the task, you must realize that you are already covered. Coverage is not just about protecting your material possessions; it's also about protecting your mind and body. You must always remember that the most important thing to maintain in this lifetime is your mental and physical health. A fortune can't be materialized without the vessel, so you must remain available and keep your mind open toward gratitude and peace, so that when you clear out the negative self-talk in your mind, you can allow the sparks of inspiration and motivation to grow and move you into spiritual action. As you learn to remain flexible and not allow your problems to break and destroy you, then you can start adopting the practice of bending but not breaking.

Bend But Don't Break

During my service in the Airforce, I had to learn the importance of flexibility and staying committed to the mission, regardless of the situation. You must have faith in the system to deliver the right results and stay loyal when the process fails. It prepares you to plan for multiple outcomes, to create a strategy that is flawless. The problem is that you can't influence what is outside of your control. This can easily cause tension between you and the work environment, but the beauty in the stress it causes is a learned habit of patience and perseverance. As you ascend to cruising altitude, it will be crucial on how you handle external and internal pressure from associates and family alike.

The external pressure will come by everyone asking for your time and attention, drawing you away from your personal mission and tasks, but it will be up to you to discern between who adds to your goals and who subtracts from them. An important question to ask yourself is, "Who is always there when I need help and support?" As you give love and support to others, it should be reciprocated equally to you as well. The world is going to pull you in multiple directions, with a flood of information and peer pressure, to believe the narrative of lack and scarcity, so this will be the time when you will depend on your angels, mentors, and support network for guidance and direction.

The internal pressure may prove to be an even bigger challenge, depending on who you are and how you handle stress. It will come in the form of negative self-talk and self-limiting thoughts that cause drifting. Most people in this world are unaware of the way they think, and they allow themselves to lose sight of the mission and go off course, until life deals them a heavy blow. A question you will need to ask is, "What things do I tell myself that don't serve me anymore?" This simple exercise will focus your mind to see when you are getting in your own way, and change your behavior.

The good news is that you are still in a position to win, despite all the pressure around you. The human spirit is resilient by nature, and our need to survive forces us to seek solutions, giving you positive and negative options to overcome your challenges. Your positive options will ensure that your mental and emotional health stay intact when you believe everything is going wrong. It is natural to feel overwhelmed with the forces outside of your control, but as you start to figure out how you cope with stress, you can begin to look for the triggers that set you off, so that you achieve your own version of self-mastery.

My own desire for excellence leads me to become my own worst critic, always thinking of a way to improve and perfect my craft. As I started to learn about the internal pressure that affects me, I knew what area to seek help in, which gave me more freedom to explore my thoughts and find the triggers that put me in that negative space. The challenges I face today are more advanced compared to what I dealt with 10 years ago, but the internal pressure was the same, slowing me down from accomplishing my goals sooner. Now I am more prepared to expect how I react to roadblocks, and I ask myself the right questions sooner, to liberate my mind to get back into focus. As you begin to explore the way you see the world, and your perception changes about the people you surround yourself with, you will develop the positive behavior of having positive self-talk, and thoughts of abundance, in order for you see the good in every situation. Just remember to always make time for at least 10 minutes of meditation per day. Seek the necessary help to guide you toward a process of growth, and detach yourself from the result, saving you from internal stress, to strengthen yourself to handle the external stress outside of your control.

The Work Never Ends

In order to overcome fear, you must lose yourself in the service of others. This is because you continuously involve yourself in action, so you don't have to think about your self-limiting beliefs. This can develop a longtime habit for you so that you can understand the value of committing your life to something that is bigger than yourself. There is the sad truth of how quickly a person's life disappears when they retire from their careers, because they have nothing left to look forward to, and as they drift aimlessly through the rest of their lives, they begin to waste away because the feeling of complacency has taken over. You must understand that if you are still living and breathing on this earth, then your work is never done. There is always someone that you can mentor and teach about your life's journey and your occupation, to pass your experience on to the next person.

It is my belief that work ethic can be developed once you find the desire to strive for excellence within your craft. As humans, we were created to build. Whether in the physical or mental space, we have been given the innate ability to construct ideas, and manifest them into their physical counterpart. As a spiritual being, your life's work may not lie in a job or occupation, but may depend on the renewal of the minds of others around you.

I had to face the reality that I will always work until the day I leave. To serve and accept responsibility doesn't mean that my life will become stale, but the discipline that I commit myself to will liberate me from the negative forces that try to pull away my focus. The biggest mental shift I have to make, from a boy to a man, is to become accountable for my actions, commit myself to working every day toward a goal, put childish things away that delay my spiritual growth, and begin to see each day as a single building block to build my kingdom. You begin to see the big picture, and you realize that an empire was not built in a day. Then you can live stress free, knowing that a daily commitment to your dreams and goals will manifest the result you seek; but it's not necessarily holding a specific result in your mind, but the destination that you desire to go to, through the result that you are seeking.

The enemy will seek to keep you off of your path by distracting you with material possessions, an overwhelming number of social activities, power, ego, and many other vices that will encourage you to delay finding out who you truly are. It is with these tools that people become drifters in life, and as they lack direction, they lack the focus to resist the temptations of life. Being able to commit yourself to a life of work isn't just about having a daily routine; it is also about keeping you sharp and on top of your game when no one is pushing you to do more. The undeniable trait of a legend within his or her industry is the fact that they always spend time alone to perfect their skills. While everyone else may be out enjoying life, they burn the midnight oil and have an obsessive desire to always be better.

If you want to create a legacy for yourself, and become a legend in your craft, you must accept this fact of life, and find the silver lining from separating yourself from the masses. Never forget that in order to live the life the others can't, you must do the things today that others won't—this is the idea of hard work and discipline when you feel that you have achieved everything possible. Success is unique, based on everyone's interpretation of happiness. When you look at yourself in the mirror and look back on the years of your life, will you suffer from the regret of failure, or will you have the joy of achievement? Take a minute to think about the events that have led you up to this moment, and ask yourself what you are looking forward to, because if you do not like the days that lie ahead, then you must change something in your present.

The Best Days Are Ahead

Everyone likes to look at life from a rearview mirror, but they forget that the best view is ahead of them. If you lived a life that is similar to mine, you will notice that your high school and college friends will always try to live in their *glory days*, the wonderful time of life where responsibilities were low, and people were at the peak of their social life on campus. For some people, those were the best days of their lives, because that's when they had the most notoriety, and they even built their reputations based on what they did during school. But what does that mean for the rest of their lives?

You may see the star athletes or the cool kids from school, years from now, and discover that they live a life of quiet desperation, grasping at the memories that they left behind, not understanding the value of reinventing themselves. It can be the present for some people because they didn't have the foresight to think about who they want to be tomorrow, and their present moment is filled with complacency and mediocrity. It is important not to fall for this same trap, handcuffing yourself to memories and not to dreams. This is where it is imperative that you change your perspective, from looking back into the past to looking forward into the future. As creators, we can change the trajectory of our lives with a single choice, and with that choice is the possibility of becoming somebody totally different than who you were as a child.

Pride and ego cloud a person's vision, making them think that they have become everything they intended to be; but if you humble yourself and begin to think outside of your comfort zone, you will see your past experiences or preparation for your next journey.

As a teenager in high school, I was never content with the person that I was; I was always looking at what I could do to improve myself in the future. I couldn't understand why most of my peers didn't think this way. And even though I was not the smartest kid or the most athletic, I knew in the back of my mind that I could always improve and challenge myself to do more, and there was an inherent desire to be better than who I was yesterday.

You may find that few of your friends will support you in your endeavors, but that's okay; it will be strangers that now become your biggest supporters to assist you in your journey. It will take a team effort for you to reach your wildest fantasies, so it will be important that you always look toward the future to see what you can improve on, what tools you can learn, and how you need to position yourself to allow your hard work to pay off. Whether you are a star athlete, a student, class president, or employee of the month, there is always something to look forward to in this life. The day that you start looking backwards is the day you start to fall behind. It's very important to use the past to learn the lessons from the mistakes that you made, and to nurture the relationships that you established. But when you start to look at it as a lifestyle and not a learning tool, you will fall for the same trick that the majority of people are victim to.

Allow the 7 navigators to open your mind to wonder about yourself and the people you surround yourself with, because with one decision, you have the ability to change everything around you, and to bring opportunities into your life that will benefit you and your family forever. This can be very difficult for some people, because you must decide who is most important to you in your life, and where to concentrate your focus in order to benefit them. It is my hope that you choose to serve society, your family, and your community, avoiding your ego that will drive you back to the past, where nothing can be changed. The future can look bright for all of us, but we must choose to be the light that shines in the darkness. Despite popular opinion, you can live a life of abundance by doing the right things, because the Universe rewards you in the future for doing the right thing today.

On the Horizon

A final word of encouragement for you in your journey will be to look to the stars as a hope for a better tomorrow. As you open your mind to the true possibilities of life, allow the 7 navigators to lead you on a journey of exploration and discovery. The aim that you should aspire to reach is to renew your view of life every few years as you learn and grow from your pain and pleasure. We are never guaranteed tomorrow; and because of this, it is all within your power to choose a better life for yourself. We seldom think about the long-term effects of the simple choices we make daily, and it is my hope that you begin to look at the precious moments you get to share with friends and family, as you see the light within yourself that you can share with the rest of the world. You have a light that shines bright to others, and no matter how you see the world around you, the true goodness of life will be shown despite you.

As our most valuable asset on this side of existence, time will always tell you the true story about everything you involve yourself in. It was in Fayetteville, North Carolina, in 2012, where I was shown the path to my own personal potential, and the years that followed have been rewarding within each challenge I faced in my personal and professional life. But looking back at it all gave me hope to become the example for others to follow, and never to be satisfied with an average way of life. If it is your desire to grow and seek the true knowledge of the Universe, it will take a process of letting go of who you used to be, to accept the man or woman that you are destined to be in the future.

It can be scary at times because nothing is certain until we are knee deep in each experience, and when the lesson becomes clear, we must cope with the results and detach ourselves from the endless possibilities that we could have changed. The circle of life will always give you an opportunity to make things right when you have done wrong, so stay vigilant and prepare yourself for the chances you have before you, and keep an open heart and mind to change the narrative and write the ending to your story. Always remember that wisdom, knowledge, understanding, counsel, might, and the fear of your creator are the key ingredients to live in the spirit of your creator; and everything begins with the true essence of the creation of love.

If you choose to love something, you are deciding to show empathy and compassion for that person or circumstance, and you are detaching yourself from receiving that love back. When you begin to think of life as a means of giving your love away and expecting nothing in return, then you are at a level of freedom that most people dream about. To make things simpler for you, try to think of life in another person's shoes, and look at the way you would react if they were in your position. This shift in your mind will allow you to seek a higher path than what you see around you in the world, and you will be able to look beyond that person's hatred and prejudice, and see that they are simply a soul that needs healing.

Please understand that living in the spirit of your creator will not make you a perfect person; you will always have times when you will make mistakes and slip back to a previous version of yourself, but becoming aware of the thoughts that come into your mind will allow you to detach yourself from them, and you will always be able to return your thoughts to the creative space of loving your fellow man or woman. If you commit your life to this way of thinking, then you'll become open to finding new opportunities to open up your spiritual path, and you will begin new journeys during your lifespan that will expose your light to a bigger audience around the world. Whether you aspire to be world famous, or to simply raise a family and live a simple life, it is a shared responsibility for all of us to stand up for the goodness in this world, and to never allow evil to take over our lives.

Conclusion

A few questions I would like to leave you with deal with opening the channels of spiritual energy, to maintain balance in your life, and bring you peace during your meditations:

Surrender your fears – What do you fear the most?

Release your guilt – What do you blame yourself for?

Release your shame – What are your biggest disappointments in yourself?

Release all your sadness and loss – What do you grieve?

Release your denials within yourself – What lies do you tell yourself?

Release all illusions in yourself – What ideas cause separations to exist between you and the world?

Release all attachments – What material things do you attach yourself to?

The 7 Navigators

These ideas, in meditative practice, are known as the 7 chakras, and they are our entry into the spiritual Universe. When you begin to practice self-observation, it is my hope that these 7 questions will open up the doors of opportunities that you seek, and spark a new lifestyle that will break generational curses and behaviors that are blocking you from reaching cruising altitude. Peace be with you.

Conclusion

As a free bonus, Steve is offering a free 30-minute consultation to instruct readers on developing a game plan for using the 7 Navigators for personal growth and fulfillment. To contact him please visit www.Navigator7.com, and mention this page to schedule your consultation today!

Follow "The 7 Navigators" on Instagram and Facebook for daily inspiration and content from Steve himself.

The 7 Navigators

Quotation Sources:
Source: https://www.familyfriendpoems.com/ poem/if-by-rudyard-kipling

Made in the USA
Columbia, SC
02 November 2024